Get Real, Ladies

Get Real, Ladies

CAREER CHALLENGES, CHANGES & CHOICES

Kim DeCoste

1.   Business & Economics / Careers
2.   Business & Economics / Women

VOLUME ORDERS: Companies, professional groups, club, and other organizations may qualify for special terms when ordering quantities of this title. For information, please contact Kim@DeCosteAssociates.com

ISBN: 0996562400
ISBN 13: 9780996562409
Library of Congress Control Number: 2015910628
Dauntless Resources, Centennial, CO

Additional information can be found at www.GetRealCareerBook.com

I dedicate this book to my family, especially to the women in my life who have shown, by their examples, the importance of working both in the home and throughout their careers. They have always inspired me and made me exceptionally proud. Especially my mother, Diane, but also Lori, Marcia, Jennifer, Catharina, Stephanie, Brynna, Lindsay, Michele, Duffy, Creagh, and my grandmothers, Beatrice, Estelle, Beverly, and Ollie—each of these women has raised or is raising children, has been or still is extraordinarily supportive of her husband, and has taught me through her grace and grit what "ladylike" really means. And to Kathleen and Caitlin, who are free spirits with enormous capacities to give to others, I can't leave you out just because you are not married with children!

To my girlfriends who have been so incredibly supportive over the years, thank you for helping me keep my sanity and for your encouragement as I wrote this book.

And finally, to my boys—my husband, Paul, and my son, Stephen—thank you for letting me pursue this dream and for your endless support. I love you.

Contents

Introduction

> The greatest madness a man can be guilty of in
> this life, is to let himself die outright, without being
> slain by any person whatever, or destroyed by any
> other weapon than the hands of melancholy.
> — MIGUEL DE CERVANTES SAAVEDRA, *DON QUIXOTE*

This book has been my dream and a work in progress for several years. I drafted the first outline in a journal while traveling in 2010. The idea is to (hopefully) continue with the "get real" theme and explore careers, industries, and the unique challenges and changes in several areas and for particular subsets of people. I have been working in employment or recruitment in one form or another almost my entire career, starting as a headhunter (technical recruiter for an agency) in Los Angeles in the early '90s. I have interviewed, hired, placed, and advised thousands of people over the years, and I have seen some crazy things related to careers and decision-making.

I firmly believe the opportunity to work in some form or another is one of the most fundamental needs and potential pleasures in life. It is eternally gratifying to be productive and fairly compensated and to feel self-value. Not everyone is able to experience that feeling, however, and for far too many people, work is a necessary evil that diminishes quality of life and feels like a burden. Certainly there are instances when work is "just a job" (especially early in our careers). Everyone has to pay his or her dues. But as we mature and have choices and options, too often we coast blindly through the crossroads and do not stop, take stock, take charge, and accept ownership for our own work and well-being.

The work-related challenges people face and the elusive, if not impossible, notion of work-life balance are not unique to women, but this first book is directed to the female audience. I just think there is a huge need for honest conversation among women and for their own good—giving them a chance to examine their situations, evaluate choices, and explore opportunities for change.

The goal of this book is to get that conversation started. I want to spark inspiration through the tales of others and what they have achieved. The women featured here are everyday women who, in my view, have accomplished extraordinary successes. They are some of the people I personally have looked to for inspiration when I have doubted myself. I feel so fortunate to be surrounded by such individuals, and I am eternally grateful for the time and energy that each has put into supporting me in this project.

I did not want to create a workbook. I never like to write in my own books, and the things you might want to write as you go along here are personal and will change over time. My suggestion is that you grab a notebook or small journal, because in a few instances I ask you to consider points and jot notes to yourself. This book is not a how-to manual. It is not the definitive guide on career change. It is a book that is intended to inspire and spark action. It is intended to help you see yourself, your options, and your potential more clearly and to see (as you will read many times) that I believe "if she can do it, why can't I?"

It was Chinese philosopher Lao-Tzu (571–531 BC) who wrote, "A journey of a thousand miles begins with a single step."

So let's go, ladies.

CHAPTER 1

The Real Myths

I have been absolutely terrified every minute of
my life—and I have never let it keep me from
doing a single thing I wanted to do.
—GEORGIA O'KEEFFE

t is time to pull the curtain away and finally say it like it is. In some form or another, work is part of every person's life. Whether we like it or not, work defines us—even the lack of work can define us. Not everyone feels the same way about working in general, and not everyone agrees regarding the extent of its importance; but like it or not, when we grow up, eventually we work.

As women, thankfully—now more than in past generations—we continue to see increasing numbers of options. Clearly it's not yet a perfect world with respect to some aspects of equality, such as pay or even access to some kinds of opportunities. Nonetheless, I believe it is fair to say a little girl can assume that when she grows up, few things, personally or professionally, will be off-limits based on her gender. Certainly she can reasonably aspire to be just about anything; at this point, only a few lofty goals remain elusive to us.

That said, how do we decide what we want to be when we grow up? When do we decide it? I believe these are pivotal questions we must ask our daughters, and we must ask early and often. Too many women approach work haphazardly. And with women being especially good at adapting and changing for others, many women all over the world—not just in the United States—stumble into a career path and follow it arbitrarily to its natural conclusion. In addition, they often repeat that process over time. We like to pride ourselves on being flexible and adaptable, particularly if we end up raising a family, so we don't always take ownership of our career journeys the way that men do. Now, please understand, *this is fundamentally the opposite of what the most **successful** people do.* We will dig deeper into this concept in later chapters, but I believe it is a foundational point for this book.

Even today, generations removed from the equal rights movement of the seventies, young women and girls usually rush into their futures with little forethought. Then, there is the greater problem: *nobody really tells us what working life is going to be like.*

Maybe you got to go on a "take your daughter to work" day. Maybe you did an internship in school. If you are lucky, someone in your circle of family or friends is in the field you are pursuing and can offer some insight. But even these snapshots are not enough to prepare us for what lies ahead.

Then, ironically, we women are often also at the helm of a family and are faced with the choices we all make about marriage and children. With that, obviously, come additional variables. Most often, we are the ones who, by choice, take a backseat and spend at least some time having and raising our babies, if we can. If we cannot spare the time (or money), we still bear the children and then begin the insane process of pursuing the ideal work-life balance. This, I must say, is a great peeve of mine. Women are led to believe that there is an elusive balance, which implies that work and life will all somehow fall into place. Again, *nobody really tells us what working life is going to be like.*

For those who do have a plan—and I greatly admire those who do—and pursue it, things are not really much different, however. They still march into their futures with little idea of the realities of their chosen field and the challenges they will face. I personally did not have a plan and have always been a bit jealous of those who did. I admire people who thought they knew what they wanted to be and then went about the task of becoming whatever it was. Doctor. Lawyer. Teacher. Florist. Housewife. Whatever. But—perhaps you recognize a pattern—*nobody really tells us what working life is going to be like.*

And, by the way, this is also true in many cases for men. I do not want to alien-ate any male readers by jumping on a feminist bandwagon that communicates a "woe is me" attitude. However, for the purposes of this book, this time around I really do want to talk to the women. Someone has to. We have to grow up and take ownership of our lives, our choices, our careers, and ourselves, and we need to get real. I do not want to sound flip about this. It is one of the hardest—if not *the* hardest—things we will ever do. Since the beginning of time, it seems, at least in the American culture, most women and girls are given quite specific parameters for how to behave and deal with life and its challenges. We will talk about these expectations in greater detail later.

At the end of the day, however, we all have only one go-around. We have only one chance at this beautiful, crazy thing called life, in a fixed amount of time, and we must learn as fast as we can how to own and best live it. It will not be a perfect adventure free of tragedies and mistakes and disappointment. But if we are very lucky and very careful, we may have the great privilege of living a life of few regrets. That has always been a goal of mine, and that is what I hope to share here. You can create and execute a vision of your life so that, at the end of your journey, you are not filled with thoughts of what might have been.

Real Inspirations

For most of my life, I have collected quotations and inspirational books. I have volumes of handwritten journals that I treasure—journals that I kept as a teenager and young woman with passages lovingly copied from favorite books, movies, music, and poems. I have always found magic in written words and have held excellent writers in the highest esteem. It is stunning to me that some people have the ability to tie the right string of words together in such a way that, years after they were written or spoken, they still carry the magical ability to compel us in one way or another. I am inspired by them still and love to revisit these journals and reflect on what I was thinking about when I captured them.

As I have gotten older, it has become harder to keep up my collection. I used to lie on my bed for hours and copy things as a form of relaxation. I no longer have the luxury of that kind of quiet time. However, I still keep a running document on my computer, and I copy and paste passages into it when I stumble onto something good.

At this busy point in my life, I find that I am most often inspired by *people*. Now, however, I find I am most inspired by their actions, by their willingness to take risks, and by their resilience. Over the past seven years, since first launching my company, DeCoste & Associates, LLC, I have been consistently inspired by the people around me who are willing to chase a vision of themselves—a dream, perhaps—and who have the tenacity to realize those dreams. Their example makes me think, "Well, if s/he can do it, then maybe I can too."

Many of those people's stories are in this book. I am profoundly grateful to all of these women for sharing their experiences with me for this project. I feel lucky to have landed where I did when I did. I have had the great fortune to meet, work with, observe, and get to know most of these women personally. The list, by the way, is long. There are so many extraordinary people out there! Think of the human-interest stories seen on the evening news. Every single day, all around the world and right down the street, there are people just like you and me who are taking big risks and doing great things.

Real Myths

Not too long ago, I was invited to a party at which all attendees were women. It was a good mix of people, but by the end of the evening, I was shocked at the pervasive sense of dissatisfaction among them. Several women were the main breadwinners in their households, and most of the women were high earners. All had lovely homes, good marriages, and healthy kids. Yet few seemed really satisfied and happy.

Many joked about needing their wine to get through most days. Several compared the side effects of various antidepressant medications. They talked about feeling unwell, sleeping poorly, and other maladies. It was eye opening to me for a couple of reasons. One, sadly, was that I realized I was not feeling great, yet was neither alone nor in the worst condition. The second was that everyone there had something to complain about, making me wonder about the general condition in which women find themselves these days.

Going back to my upbringing and education, by the seventies and eighties, many things had changed or were really finally beginning to change. We look back and see examples of all kinds of firsts for women as a direct result of the equal rights movement of the sixties. By the time I was in middle school, women functioned in corporate roles, in political leadership roles, as astronauts. We believed we really could be anything we wanted to be. In my case, I was also lucky to have parents—particularly a mother—who encouraged me to be anything and to try anything and believed I could succeed at anything I wanted to do. This was true for most of the women I know today.

But as we have climbed the ranks in our respective career areas, what have we found? We still find a bumpy road, in many cases, with male colleagues who are often resistant to us as peers or superiors. We still put up with discriminatory and demeaning behavior at times. We often have to do more to be recognized and try harder to advance. And we still do it for seventy-one cents to a man's dollar. Gender bias is real, even if the paths have been cleared. We remain determined to climb the ladders, so we push on—but at great expense. Battling upstream makes us stronger swimmers and leaves us tired when we are finished.

As is evidenced by the fact that women are starting their own businesses in greater numbers than ever, it seems that once we get to whatever the professional destination is, we shake off the glass, look around, and increasingly dislike what we see. Although that scene appears to be changing—mainly to accommodate the demands of the millennial generation as it enters the workforce—most traditional businesses still operate with fairly rigid rules that fail to help us overcome the biggest myth of all—that of work-life balance. We will come back to this later.

It is amazing to me how few companies—relatively speaking—understand that flexibility is probably the number-one benefit they could offer employees. Workers of both genders need it to make life run more smoothly. And workers who are less stressed about their personal lives can better concentrate and dedicate themselves to their tasks at work. Offering good employees flexible schedules helps them keep life in order and costs little operationally.

This myth about work-life balance, I think, causes the greatest stress for women. I understand that men have this issue as well, but in terms of what has been traditionally expected of women, *adding* work outside the home to our "given" roles as wives and mothers by definition puts a greater burden on us. We appreciate and understand that many of us—myself included—were lucky enough to marry men who are great dads and husbands and who do much more than their predecessors did around the house to keep the family running smoothly. That is a choice some men make. Women have fewer choices in this matter. Most do the lion's share of the housework and childcare (bathing, feeding, homework, and activities), and if they work outside the home, they have that to manage as well.

I came across an organization here in Denver called Women in the Mix (www.WomenInTheMix.com). Founded by two professional women, Cindy Chang Mahlberg and Nicole Elias Seawell, Women in the Mix soundly rejects the notion of work-life balance and instead discusses the work-life mix.

This organization defines the five areas in which women operate—work, family, house, self, and community—and puts forth on its website the notion that "the concept of work-life balance is a misnomer because it implies a dichotomy, with work on one side and life on the other, and that there is a point where it all delicately teeters in equilibrium. Such an analogy leads many on a futile and frustrating search for an elusive 'balance.' Women in the Mix strives to shift the conversation so that individuals focus on the entirety of their lives and are empowered to make informed choices to create a thriving work-life mix at each stage of life."

I found this approach completely illuminating and so refreshing. Alas! There is no perfect balance to be achieved. And by breaking down those five areas, they help us see what the juggling act really consists of. I had not considered how much I was struggling to maintain all five equally. Neither, I guess, do those women friends I mentioned at the beginning. The "self" part rarely makes it to the top of the to-do list. Many women also suffer from a severe lack of community, with work and family consuming all the energy they have to give. So I think this revelation of the five areas in which women operate helps us to see what we need to focus on and may help us to better balance ourselves over time.

The single biggest myth, however, that I think keeps us all spinning in circles is the notion of equal. By definition, this term has it all wrong, with *equal* defined in the dictionary as being the same in quantity, size, degree, or value. Okay, I will concede value with some caveats later, but men and women are not equal in those or most other measures. In fact, we are entirely different. We know this inherently, yet we women insist on trying to be equal. It will not work because, with few exceptions, we were programmed by the Infinite to be different. That was the goal.

So rather than trying to be equal, perhaps we can try to be better—on different terms. We can find success in all aspects of our lives without worrying about being equal to men, being true to ourselves individually instead. The term *individually* is absolutely the operative word here. My definition of success is probably not exactly the same as yours. In fact, I don't know too many people who share their definition of success with anyone except, if they are lucky, perhaps their spouse.

Think about it. What would true success look like for you? (I promised myself that this book would not be a workbook with lines to fill in, so grab a small journal or notebook and think about how you define success for yourself.) Here are some elements to consider.

1. Work outside the home: What would you do? What would your title be? Would you work full-time? How much money would you take home? Would you manage others?
2. Family: Would you have children? How many? How involved with their lives would you be? How successful would they be in school? What activities would they participate in that required your help (transportation, funding, coaching, for example)? Would you be married? How would your love life be?
3. Community: Would you be involved with your community? Church? Politics? How active would you be?
4. Home: Would you have domestic help? Would you do the cooking? Cleaning? Childcare? How large would your house be? What would it look like?
5. Self: Would you have hobbies? Take classes? Exercise? Travel (how often and with whom)?

Now think about what you have written down. Really look at the bar you are setting for yourself. Is it realistic? Could you achieve it? I know that my definition of success has changed radically over the past fifteen years or so, and I expect it will continue to change. The reason is that my priorities have changed.

Now, it is important here to concede a point I probably should have already made. I am blessed with the ability to have some choices in my life now, which some women do not have. However, what I would like to assert now and throughout the book is that most women have more choices than they realize. Many of us ignore or forgo choices and then look back with regret. I have spoken about this at women's conferences, and invariably people nod their heads quietly, acknowledging this fact.

We will come back to this point later, but we must take ownership of our options and acknowledge when the path of least resistance has defined our journey. It's okay that it happens. We have to prioritize, and sometimes that path is the right one. Sometimes easy is best, but we cannot have it both ways. Either we are striving or we are stagnating.

Regarding success, what we must acknowledge is that, at the end of the journey, there are two irrefutable concepts that define the choices we make. They are not glamorous terms. They are not sexy terms. However, they are at the heart of how we choose what we choose and why we do what we do. They are *prioritization* and *accountability*.

I have long believed that keeping these two terms properly aligned really is the secret to achieving goals and finding success. The example I use is a fairly simple one. In 1999, my husband and I got married. We lived in a beautiful nine-hundred-square-foot apartment in Hermosa Beach, California, with an ocean view from every window, including the shower. We paid $1,600 per month in rent, and we had a garage. That was great for a young couple in that town at that time.

Shortly after getting married, we traveled to visit his family in southern Ohio. My sister-in-law has a beautiful, large home, and we were there to celebrate a graduation. I watched my nieces and their friends coming and going and thought back to our little apartment, wondering what family life would look like there. When we got home, I watched neighborhood kids playing in the alley, and I knew that we would have to move if we were going to raise a family in the way I imagined we should. Median home prices at that time in Hermosa started at $600,000. We were doing well, but not that well.

So we started looking and put the word out. My husband was offered a position in Denver, if we would move fast, so seven weeks later, we were on our way over the Rockies to a new life. We signed a one-year lease on an apartment we had not seen before arriving and committed to finding and buying a home before the next year. It required a lot of effort from both of us. It meant that we did not fly back to see family that year for our first Christmas or Easter or summer vacation.

Finding a home was our number-one priority, and we were both fully accountable to that goal. When my mother asked why we weren't coming home, it was easy to explain that buying a home to start a family was why we had left in the first place, and we had to own the goal and save the money. She understood, of course, and we were able to move into our new house twelve months after we arrived in Denver.

I realize that sounds like a silly little story, but it is an easy one with which to prove my point about prioritization and accountability. To feel that you are succeeding in life and in work, you must know what your priorities are. Those are the areas where you measure (judge) your relative success. It is not a news flash to tell you that *it is not possible to have all things be equally important and equally successful.* It just is not. If you can define for yourself what things matter most (or what matters more than something else), then you can gauge your progress. And you must be accountable for those priorities. You cannot tell yourself that your professional success is the highest priority if you are not willing to give in some other areas to accommodate the time and energy required to achieve that success. *This dissonance is what makes us feel as if we are failing.*

The perspective of time has really informed me in this area. I have always set goals against timelines so that I could verify whether I was on track. The house-buying story is a good example. One month after we bought the house, we found out we were having a baby. We had already made some adjustments to life to prepare for this. When we'd moved out, I was still working as a technical recruiter. The economy took a turn for the worse in 2000, and the division of my company shut down our whole team. The layoff allowed me the chance to move away from work that was 100 percent commission and contingency.

I wanted to work in a more traditional nine-to-five environment, so I found a position recruiting for an online university, which seemed like a logical extension of my skills. The office was five minutes from our house, and it was an easy position that allowed me time to be home and was much less stressful than recruiting had been. The problem was, it was also less challenging. So I decided to pursue an MBA while I was there. It made work more valuable, and I felt better about being underemployed.

Once my son was born, however, everything changed. I became professionally restless and really worried about what life would be like as he got older if I continued working in the same way. I cannot adequately describe the feeling now, years later, but when I read back through my journals, I can best describe it as fear. I knew that I wanted to keep working. I liked working. But I also knew that I did not want a nanny or day care to raise my son, and I could not picture what I would do to allow me to work in any other setting. At that time, we did not have the financial security to allow me to quit and be a stay-at-home mom; I also knew that I was not programmed to be a stay-at-home mom, as much as I wished to be then. So I decided that I would find a way to start my own business by the time my son went to kindergarten.

Here is another myth: Starting a business will allow you to set your own hours and work a flexible schedule, and it will offer you freedom. I can say that starting a business is a tremendous challenge and requires tenacity and dedication like few other things in life do. It also requires enormous discipline and clear goal setting. I will come back to this later. The takeaway here is that, although I missed the goal by a year, by the time my son entered first grade, I was self-employed and working as a coach and career expert, creating curriculum and advising private individual clients. I was able to make that work for about three years until it all shifted again.

Therein lies one big lesson: as life evolves, so do goals. It is not quitting or giving up to admit that, for whatever reason, priorities change and with that so can just about everything else. The challenge is to welcome the change, accept it, realign the compass, and march wholeheartedly in the new direction without guilt or regrets. Few decisions in life are truly irreversible.

This is one of the central messages I hope to convey in this book. Change happens, and we often have to adjust our plans. That is the part of life we cannot control. What we can control is how we react to the changes and not allow them to dictate our path to success. This is not a prescriptive how-to book but rather a book with practical information as well as stories of real women who, like you and me, decided to do something for themselves that had meaning. The intention is to show you "if she can do it, so can you," because that is true.

There is not one person depicted here who comes from great privilege or had any real advantage—other than her own willingness to try. That is another key message. Each of us truly has the inner capacity to do meaningful work in a way that makes us happy. No two visions will be exactly the same, and there certainly is no one right answer. Hopefully, there is enough diversity among the women depicted here that you can find a story that resonates for you and inspires you to try.

CHAPTER 2

The Real World

Our life always expresses the result of our dominant thoughts.
—Søren Kierkegaard

We often read about those who bemoan the fact that professional security seems to be gone. This is a particularly tough reality, they say, for men. A generation ago, a motivated man might enter his career and expect to climb the ranks within an organization and retire from that same place years later, pension and gold watch in hand.

This reality does not exist anymore. It is also true that such a reality really never existed for women unless, maybe, they were teachers or nurses. In corporate life, women have clung to jobs or moved from job to job as needed, depending on the circumstances. I do not think most women have the expectation of stability that men have had. However, it seems that women do lack the motivation, in many cases, to demand change, expect growth, and seek new challenges at the same rate that men do. Perhaps it is because we are socialized to be more averse to risk. Perhaps it is just because we don't like to rock the boat. The reality of work now, however, is that it is wildly dynamic and ever changing. To stay ahead of the curve, we have to be willing to adapt, grow, and take risks.

Also, more than ever before, work intrudes on personal time. There really is little separating the time many people spend at work and the time they spend at home other than where they are sitting. Globalization and technology have put us all on a twenty-four-hour clock, and drawing the lines can be challenging.

However, we must find ways to protect the time that we do not spend working so that we can recharge and enjoy those other areas of our lives. Boundaries are important to establish and maintain.

Even through periods of self-employment, when every call matters and every contact is a potential client, I have drawn a line around the hours between 6:00 and 9:00 p.m. I tell people freely that this is "family time" and that a message left or e-mail sent will be reviewed after nine o'clock and replied to as urgently as is required. People know this about me, and it has never been a problem. I charge my phone away from my bedroom so that I do not hear it beep and ring all night. You can do this too. Nowadays, it seems we are in competition with one another to appear the most exhausted and in demand. That is a competition I do not need to win.

Beyond our phones, we have the relatively new phenomenon of social media. While some may argue that the jury is still out on the value of social media, I would say it is undoubtedly a valuable personal and professional tool. You must learn how to draw lines with social media as well, however. Not understanding the importance and risks associated with social media could end your career.

Know, too, that you cannot really use all types of social media. Many trends come and go, but a few are absolutely used for business. You need to learn about the different tools, deciding what you want to use for personal reasons and what is of value professionally. Then, it is of paramount importance that you decide how you want to be perceived. Who is the "real you" for social media? That persona becomes your personal brand to many, and it will be perceived—as you are—to be successful or not based on how you communicate.

This book could not begin to unearth all the different forms of social media. I am not enough of an expert to write that book, and it already exists. There are, in fact, numerous books to help you familiarize yourself with various social media platforms. For my purposes, I use only three and, of those, only two regularly.

Facebook has proven to be an extremely useful tool for both near and long-distance connectivity, and it allows you to control your voice and your audience. There are personal pages, and there are business pages. You can also create lists and define where you want your connections to be archived. So, for example, you can post a picture of your child to the friends and family list and the latest article from *Fast Company* to colleagues.

You may decide that distinction is not necessary and post all to everyone, but understand that such a level of transparency does come with risks. Do you really want your colleagues to see you with the fruity umbrella drink in a bathing suit on vacation? Do you want members of the business community to know where your children are for summer camp or which church you attend? Maybe you do, and, if so, that is fine, but you must be mindful that once such things are out there, they can never be fully removed.

Personally, I have opted for a high level of transparency for various reasons, but I am also very careful of (1) whose friend requests I accept and (2) what I post. The rule I use for accepting requests is the following: "Is this someone with whom I would go to coffee or grab a drink after work? Do I know this person in the real world?" If the answer is yes, then I accept the request. If I am not sure or I do not really know the person, then, of course, I do not connect.

LinkedIn remains my go-to professional site. The standards for connection here are higher. I connect only with people I know, have worked with, or have dealt with in the business community. I value my LinkedIn network and try to limit it to people I really know. As I told someone once, my LinkedIn network should include only people who I know will pick up the phone when my name comes up on caller ID.

LinkedIn is used universally by recruiters and human resource professionals. You can be active with groups that will connect you to others who have mutual interests and build your network that way as well. You can also research prospective employers, colleagues, and other interesting connections for job searches. LinkedIn allows you to search by company, so if you are conducting a job search, you can see if you or someone you know is acquainted with anyone at a prospective company and can offer an introduction.

LinkedIn also allows you to link to projects, third-party clients, and specific work. It allows you to make recommendations and get them. Do that. Use LinkedIn to endorse your acquaintances and their skills. They will reciprocate. LinkedIn has almost supplanted the need for a traditional résumé, allowing you to truncate your résumé and keep all the beautiful details online for further review.

If you use LinkedIn, make sure that your profile is available on your résumé and on any other piece of collateral that might circulate about you. Keep your LinkedIn profile current and check it regularly, especially when you are in job-search mode, to see how the profile is being seen. Tweak and improve your profile if it is not getting viewed. Again, numerous resources are available to help you if you need it.

With that all said about social media, it is my personal belief that the usefulness of job boards has greatly decreased over the years. There are sites that still have good information for specialized career needs and for people at certain levels. But the days of going to a job board and really finding a suitable job have passed, in my view. I know people still post on job boards, and some still get hired from them, but I believe you are much better off conducting a real job search and networking with real people face-to-face as much as possible. It is harder, but the results will be much better in the long run. Plus, you are building a real network this way. We will come back to the importance of a real network.

I am getting ahead of myself a bit. The real world is not just about technology tools that we all need to master. It is about life and the cards we are dealt. The women we meet in this chapter have stories of success in the face of challenges and the determination to go on despite the difficulties. Their stories are inspiring and remind us that we are stronger than we think we are. Dr. Chris Linares is a family doctor, and Paula Wiens is someone I met through the South Denver Metro Chamber of Commerce. Both ladies are models of strength, grace, and professionalism, and they are my first examples of everyday women succeeding every day.

Dr. Chris Linares

I have known Chris Linares for nearly fifteen years. I met her through our church, where, for years, my husband and I organized a chili cook-off and barbecue as a fundraiser. Chris was a standout at one of the early cook-offs because (1) she was a woman all by herself with her two daughters, and (2) she took on ribs! I remember thinking she was especially brave for choosing ribs and for bringing her girls, who were probably both approaching eight and ten or so years old. She had a great attitude and really made an impression as a positive, interesting person.

At some point, I found out that she was a doctor and was opening a new practice near our local hospital. She was just getting started, and our doctor was moving, so I thought we should give her a try. She was terrific, and I was delighted to be able to support her efforts at starting her own practice with a partner. I remember being in awe of her for her professional success. It seemed like an enormous undertaking. Over the years, we have continued to see her, and she and I have always kept a friendly rapport, though we do not currently socialize outside of the office.

What I like about Chris is that she is down-to-earth. Very real. She and I are about the same age, both have kids, both are married. We have a lot in common in terms of our outlook and some health issues. I never felt I had to exaggerate how much I do or don't exercise or downplay my love of Chardonnay. She gets it and is supportive and encouraging. I have always felt totally comfortable talking to her, even through some difficult times.

So, I thought, for this book, she could lend some perspective both from her own personal viewpoint and then as a family doctor who sees hundreds of women every year. We had a great conversation, and as is always the case, I learned a lot.

Chris's story is a good one. I had not previously known much about her personal history, but as she shared it, I realized she has certainly had her ups and downs. She was raised in Ohio and said her upbringing was normal. She had loving and supportive parents, and she knew she wanted to be a doctor from the time she was four years old. Chris was always motivated and had a clear life vision. She was going to save the world, of course.

Roadblock number one came when—after all the years of knowing what she wanted to be—she failed to get into medical school on the first try. She said, though, that she remained unwavering in her commitment to the idea. So she moved to New York City and decided to work for a year as a social worker to build her résumé for medical school and try again. She found herself in Times Square looking for people to help, and she also found herself falling in love with someone she met while she was there. That was not part of the plan, but she did not question it.

The next year, she reapplied to schools and was accepted by Howard University in Washington, DC. She moved, got settled in, and was ready to take on the world. Upon admission, she was standing in a line waiting with the other medical students for updates to various required vaccinations. She got to the window, and when asked about the date of her last period, she could not recall it. They told her to step aside, and slowly she realized how long it had been. Yes, first week of medical school and Chris discovered she was pregnant.

Her boyfriend, Jerry, was a butcher in New York. He moved to DC and helped as he could, but his hours were irregular, as were hers. She did not want to get married pregnant, so they waited until after the baby was born and then got married. Before you know it, she was pregnant again. Two babies and medical school, with residency still looming. She reflected on the time wondering how they got through it, but they did.

She ended up doing her residency back in New York. They lived in Queens for the three years, and she relied on neighbors to babysit the girls at all the odd hours she needed. Rounds started at 7:00 a.m. She had to prepare for rounds. Sometimes the girls were dropped off in their pajamas at four thirty in the morning, but it somehow worked for everyone.

At some point, the city life began to wear on them a bit. She had approximately $200,000 in loans, and she wanted more autonomy and a bit less stressful environment for the kids. Chris had a sister in Denver, and after much discussion, they decided to move to Colorado. Chris worked in a small practice for about a year and eventually decided she wanted a practice of her own. One of the doctors she had come to know and like was leaving to move to where a new hospital was being built so he could start his own practice. Chris followed him. They started out with one other partner who did not work out, and eventually Chris was the majority owner and on her own, finally.

In her practice she sees in many of us the same challenges she experiences herself; moms drag sick children in, and as they sit in the corner watching, she can see in them the exhaustion and worry. She calls it forty-year-old superwoman syndrome. She thinks most of us have it around here. Responsibility, she says, has not changed significantly for most men and women. So, even if the women do work outside of the home, in most families, traditional roles and rules apply. Women are simply doing too much, often with little or no support from their spouses.

She continued by saying that almost without exception, the women she sees rank the family (not including themselves) number one, their work number two, and themselves last. Whether for exercise or recreation of some other kind, women do not tend to make time for themselves, and that has to change for all of our sakes.

Chris thinks she does a good job of keeping things separate. Work does intrude once in a while, but that is the exception. She tries hard to make time for her girls. She also has a third daughter, Sophie, who is nine years old and keeps her mom on her toes. Chris says that, for her, success in life is a lot about perseverance. She is naturally stubborn and ambitious, so her busy life is what she expected for the most part.

"I didn't know better. I just try hard," she says. Chris works hard to prioritize and juggle the priorities, as they seem to constantly change.

Of late, the greatest challenge has been deeply personal. Chris and her husband, Jerry, have been together since the beginning, and they raised two of the three children together and were fine. When we met, I noticed right away that she did not have her ring on, and I wondered. Sadly, they have really grown apart, and the end seems inevitable. There is no real animosity, just the challenge of separating and the extra challenge of doing it in such a way as to have minimal impact on the girls, especially the youngest.

Chris admits that she is mellower now than she used to be. She is still a know-it-all, but she says she takes things in stride better than she did. She does not regret the marriage because of the girls, but she wishes she had known how important the notion of partnership really is. She wishes they had spent time talking about aligning goals and long-term plans. They dove right in and thought things would just work themselves out.

Luckily, though, Chris is practical. Two years ago, when she finally allowed herself to acknowledge her frustration with the marriage and the likelihood of its demise, she took a deep inventory of the situation and made a two-year plan. She was giving herself two years to make a decision about the marriage and to prepare. She knew she needed to make sure her finances were in order. In addition to her own remaining college loans, there would be the cost of the two oldest daughters attending college. She was working more than fourteen hours per day and needed to figure out how to scale back without negatively impacting the business. She needed to establish a better balance with work and home life for everyone's sake. And, finally, when she looked around, she realized that she needed to find some good friends. She needed a support system beyond her sisters and brothers.

I think this is one of the coolest parts of the story. It takes a lot for some of us to realize we need support. As she said, she needed confidants who were not relatives. She needed adult perspective on some of the issues she was facing, and she needed the emotional support that you can get only when you give of yourself. She added "getting friends" to the list of to-dos on her phone, where she kept her two-year plan, and set about getting some friends. She is proud to report that she now has at least two good friends who are helping her through it all. One even got her back into running, so an added benefit is that she is getting in better shape too.

The reality of Chris's work and life is normal, I think. Even though she is in a demanding and visible career, the challenges she faces are universal. The real world is not tidy, and the ups and downs we all face are more similar than different. As she looks ahead, she is optimistic that they will get through this next set of challenges, and she will come out better for it. She remains eternally optimistic. She has changed the business model in her practice so she sees fewer patients, which frees up some of her time. She has given up on trying to be supermom. She will bring the cookies or bake the cupcakes but has accepted that PTO is not her thing.

A couple of years ago, Chris's stepmother, Gayle, passed away. Gayle was an organized and accomplished woman, but Chris said that "she had a long, slow slide into death," and needless to say, that is not what any of us wants. Chris has used that memory as motivation. Watching her parents deal with the situation and how they planned and set goals and stayed in love until the end inspired her to reflect on her own life, happiness, and marriage. It made her more aware of her situation and helped her see her marriage more clearly for what it was. Chris realized she was in control of her own life and happiness and choices, and she wants the fullest life she can have.

Life is too short for a lot of regrets, she says. She chooses to admire people she knows, and she tries to emulate the strengths she sees around her. She does not feel she needs to look far for role models. Looking ahead, she continues to set short- and long-term goals of all kinds. One thing she is sure of is that she wants to be skiing when she is eighty. Apparently there is a ski club she knows for octogenarians, and she intends to be among them.

Chris believes that you have to be honest with yourself about your happiness, and you have to own your ability to change. She has more optimism than fear, and she is looking ahead with confidence. For my part, I cannot wait to see her next steps. And I kind of hope to make the friend list one of these days!

Paula Wiens

My guess is that this book will be of interest to women who are midcareer or midlife. That was the audience I envisioned and focused on as I talked to different people at different ages and stages of life both on and off the record. A *Time of Our Own*, a book by Dr. Flinor Miller Greenberg and Fay Wadsworth Whitney, informed my perspective. I had the good fortune to meet Dr. Greenberg at a chamber event back in 2009, when the book had just been published. I thought it was interesting because the book talks about the *stages* of women's lives and the different needs and challenges in each stage. It is especially focused on what the authors termed "the third third of life." I was born in 1969, so I'm still squarely in the second third, but it was this book that made me first look at women I knew in the third third and then think about what that time of life might look like for me.

Life teaches us lessons the hard way sometimes. I once read something to the effect that life has certain lessons it must teach you, and it will keep on trying until you learn them. I hope this section of the book at least sparks some thoughts for readers about what we have before us. You will learn throughout this book that I, more than some, really value plans. I like the feeling of having a plan. Certainly life has taught me that my plans do not always work. Life is bigger and more unpredictable than my plans, but I still like to have them.

For women, I believe it is vital that we be honest about what life generally will look like for us when we get to the third third. We are blessed with resources and information and, for most of us, with lifestyles much different from the lifestyles of our mothers, their mothers, and their mothers before them. We live longer than women have ever lived in history. We are generally healthier than we have been in past generations. We have access to health care (generally) that prolongs life and helps us avoid diseases that would have killed us not long ago. Our husbands and partners live longer, too, but not as long as we do. Our children and parents have different needs than they had generations ago. Many middle-aged women are supporting both young adult children and parents who are senior citizens either in their own homes or indirectly through care and financial resources. This is, of course, both a blessing and a curse. How do we plan for all of that? How do we plan for ourselves, not to mention the others in our lives?

Certainly I do not have all the answers; I just know it is a conversation we must have, and I believe we have to think about all of the resources we will need to navigate these challenges. Such resources include money and access to work if we want or need it, health care, affordable housing, transportation or a lifestyle that does not require planning for it, faith, family, and friends. We need a network of support to help us along the way as we prepare, and we need to look to others for help, guidance, cautionary tales, and advice.

None of us is in this alone unless we allow ourselves to be. This topic could be a book on its own, but it is not the main theme here. Here I want to share the story of one woman I know who has faced many of these issues and is still standing strong and will come out ahead. Paula Wiens is a great example of another extraordinary, yet ordinary, everyday woman in my universe who has helped me see and understand some of life's challenges a bit better.

Paula is about the same age as my mother, by the way. My mother also married young. She also went through the end of a marriage early and then rebuilt a life with my stepfather that has been full of great ups and downs. Paula has a similar story. I think that is why Paula was of interest to me; she reminds me of my mother but with a different twist.

One thing that strikes me, as I think about Paula and other women I know who are in this stage of life, is that for all they have accomplished—and they have accomplished a lot—they do not have the same level of confidence that I see in women my age. I don't know if that is generational or a coincidence, but it seems true. Despite success and health and beauty, many still doubt themselves, or are at least far less likely to be assertive in the way that women of my generation and subsequent generations seem to be. Maybe it is because they lived through the era of the equal rights movement? Maybe it is a coincidence that I see this in Paula and my mother, but I note it time and again with women their age. In cases where a younger woman might overstate her ability or accomplishment, women such as my mom and Paula seem to understate. But that is also part of their charm.

I believe Paula's story is a common one. She grew up in a changing time when some women were getting ready to grab the brass rings while others were happy to simply follow the examples set for them by their mothers as wives and homemakers.

Raised with two younger siblings in Tucson by educators, Paula was a member of her high school modern dance troupe and a cappella choir, and she spent a year in New Zealand as an exchange student. Homesick after her senior year abroad, she declined her acceptance to San Francisco State to attend Ft. Lewis College in Durango so she could be close to her family, who had relocated to Cortez, Colorado. When her roommate, Sandy (and best friend to this day), learned that popular Durango folk singer Dean Davis was looking for a female vocalist, she told him about Paula's abilities as overheard while she sang in the shower. They connected harmoniously, but Paula was struck with stage fright.

Dean moved to Ft. Collins with his family to pursue his master's degree at Colorado State University, where Paula's parents had found teaching positions. Dean asked Paula to reconsider singing with him, so she transferred to CSU, once again to be close to her family. Paula overcame her stage fright performing with Dean at area nightclubs while attending school by day. The duo evolved into a foursome, playing gigs at regional colleges and pubs. Following an audition with the USO, the Dean Davis Company was sent on two six-week tours to Southeast Asia, performing at military hospitals and bases in Japan, South Korea, the Philippines, and Vietnam. They were helicoptered into firebases and experienced war firsthand—and, on a couple of occasions, raced from stage to bunker to escape incoming rounds.

As life would have it, Paula met a fellow student and fell in love; as she put it, she was "looking to be taken care of." She married at age twenty-one—the same time her beloved father left his "perfect family" and turned his kids' worlds upside down. When Paula's husband was offered a fellowship at Northern Arizona University, she gave up her singing career and tagged along. She had graduated from Colorado State University with a degree in anthropology but, ironically, questioned her writing abilities until a professor commented that he looked forward to her essays because they were "clearly written, concise, and easy to follow." Those kudos stuck with her when, unable to find a job in her field when the couple moved to Phoenix, Paula got a seasonal position as assistant to the PR director for the Arizona Stock Show. That led to her becoming an advertising copywriter for a regional department store chain.

Paula and Al became parents of a son, Luke, and soon after jumped on a business opportunity with her pal Sandy and Sandy's husband in Vail. Paula found part-time work with Vail Associates while her husband was on the road earning a living.

When a friend coaxed her to attend auditions for a community theater production of *Grease,* she landed the role of Sandy. Paula hadn't seen the recently released movie version and didn't even realize who Sandy was! The musical was a hit—even Betty Ford attended, accompanied by her Secret Service agent. Paula came out from under her husband's long shadow and immersed herself in Vail's performing arts community.

With renewed confidence, she got the courage to leave her troubled thirteen-year marriages. She supported Luke—the joy of her life—as an account executive with the local radio station. Paula was bright, beautiful, creative, and hardworking. She managed to hold things together for the two of them for quite a while. But as luck would have it, the economy tanked and her rent doubled. She realized that staying in Vail wasn't practical and that she'd find a more affordable life and more work opportunity if she moved to Denver.

The Mile-High City brought the visibility, connectivity, and opportunity she had hoped for. During her sales stint at a classical radio station, she met Holly Arnold, owner of Arnold Media Services and daughter of restaurateur, Sam Arnold—founder of the renowned family-owned restaurant, The Fort. Holly offered her a position as account manager for The Fort and another family-owned company, Schomp Automotive. The Schomp family has been prominent in Denver for four generations, and working with Lisa Schomp became a cornerstone of her career that has lasted to date.

Paula reflects positively on this period of her career. It was foundational to the person she is now and the work she still does. Predictably, however, as a single mother, she never felt she was doing enough for her son. He had some challenges in school, and although she did what she could at every turn, being a single working mother was no easier in the early '90s than it is now. She still has regrets about day care and time away from Luke and feels guilt at not having done more, though he has turned out to be a fine and successful young man.

After eight years as a single mom learning to live and thrive on her own, she met her second husband on a blind date. Duane was the charming and talented owner of a leading graphic design firm. The promise of companionship, stability, love, and a role model for her son were too much to resist, so Paula married again. Over time, with Duane's support, she left Arnold Media to form her own one-woman agency. She was able to work selectively, focusing on such diverse clients as Schomp Automotive, BeauJo's, and Drums Along the Rockies (drum corps competition). She even served as part-time executive director of a public education foundation.

Paula had become a talented marketing specialist with strong advertising and communication skills, poise, presence, and excellent connectivity in the community. She was able to bring positive attention and press to the causes and businesses she supported. Her son grew up, moved on with his life, and found his way. Things were going well around the time I met her in 2009. She impressed me immediately, and I knew we would be connected.

Once again, though, life threw a curve ball at Paula. Her husband's health and financial challenges took a toll on their marriage, resulting in their separating after twenty-three years. Duane is following a different path as a gifted Russian impressionist painter; the two remain good friends.

Life also took a tragic turn when Paula's younger brother died on Christmas Day in 2011 (their mom's birthday). This created all of the sad and practical problems for the family that come with the unexpected. Paula handled the logistics and details of his estate. Then her mother eventually needed assisted living. Paula had always been close to her mom, so the guilt and worry associated with this change has been hard for her, but she has managed.

Now she finds herself reinventing life once again. She is not afraid, she says, though she does wish things had played out differently, and she, like each of us, can find a million times when she wishes the ball had bounced differently. But she does not characterize these as regrets. She quipped, "You only go around once." She's still going around!

Paula is on her own again but with experience to guide her. She is navigating her mom's situation carefully and visits her regularly. She is still working, though a bit less than she used to. Clearly, she wishes she had more of a nest egg and knows she has to keep working. But at least she can. She has clients who have trusted her for almost three decades, and she considers that a great blessing. Her financial advisor assures her, "It is never too late," so she is planning for retirement...someday. Her focus is now on goal setting. She has a take-charge attitude about all of the things she can control so that she does not get blindsided by anything predictable. It's a much more empowered stance than she has had in the past. Fear sometimes creeps up on her, but she keeps it at bay.

Paula is proud of her son and the success he now enjoys. She is also proud of her career and the client relationships she has built, and she believes her success has been the ability to stay independent for so many years. Even if it was the road less traveled, she is glad to have done it. There have been trade-offs and a few regrets, but she is mostly positive.

Asked what she would tell her twenty-five-year-old self, Paula has lots to offer: (1) Live on your own when you are young. (2) Have confidence in yourself first and foremost. (3) Know that everything really does happen for a reason. (4) Learn how to manage money and meet with a financial planner. (5) Get advice on practical life decisions. Learn how to deal with contracts, rental agreements, car maintenance, and so on. (6) Think about your career, and don't give up on dreams. (7) Travel. (8) Never stop learning...life's an adventure!

Paula's journey, like that of each of us, is still under way. She is navigating new and familiar roads just by virtue of the fact that she's been at it awhile. But the optimism and courage I see in her restore my faith that we can all make it through with grace and grit and find a version of life that we can be proud of and happy to live.

CHAPTER 3

The Real You

Put an ear down close to your soul and listen hard.
—Anne Sexton

Undoubtedly, the hardest and most vital aspect of the whole process involved with understanding and planning the career change process is true introspection and honesty through self-discovery.

Who we are is a much more difficult question to answer than you might think. We are made up of myriad ever-changing components that are a combination of knowledge, interests, and abilities along with personality, personal history, experiences, hope, expectations, religion, habits, and more. These fluctuating characteristics define not only who we are but also how we assess our own sense of self and of success. For the most part, they are beyond our conscious control. Understanding these elements of ourselves will help determine what we are naturally inclined to do as well as what we are able to do—and, further, what we will enjoy doing. These are the main factors that will, ultimately, gauge our overall happiness with our choices. Finding career choices that truly make us happy is the ultimate goal.

Throughout your life and career, there will be changes imposed by external factors. The issues of spouses, children, extended family, and others often interfere with your own. Sometimes they even dictate or partially determine the choices we have or that we must make. But that is not always the case. *Taking ownership of choices is an important part of the process.* It is easy to say in retrospect that we did what we had to do for others, but it is rarely entirely true. Our lives are influenced by those other people but must not be dictated by them. To have full autonomy, professionally speaking, we must relinquish the temptation to void ourselves of responsibility. Often we take the path of least resistance, and sometimes that is the issue. Doing what we really want to do or changing the situation in which we find ourselves most often requires additional effort.

Getting real with ourselves is one of the hardest things we will ever have to do. We cannot lie to ourselves, for one thing. We *know* how we really feel, and we know when we are trying to make ourselves feel good and it is not working. With our work lives, somehow we often find ways of selling out on happiness. Too often, it seems we have come to believe that money is the most important thing. And, truly, sometimes it has to be the priority. People who are the sole or main providers for the family must work, but what other choices are they making that determine how much they must work?

Is your lifestyle a priority that makes hating the work you do for more than forty, fifty, or sixty hours per week really worth it? Could your life be simplified so that you do not have such a substantial income requirement? Would that allow you some career flexibility, enabling you to find a position that you enjoy more, even if it pays less? It comes back to that question of prioritization and accountability.

You and your family must decide what matters most and at what price. What are the greatest priorities? You might be surprised to find out that your family would gladly trade some of what you are working so hard for just to have more time with you or more time together as a family. Maybe less expensive cars or clothes or hobbies would make a difference. Who knows? If you talk about it, you might find that they do not even enjoy those things as much as you think they do.

We hear stories like this often when life imposes change on people. The economic downturn of the 2000s hit many families hard. In some cases, both parents found themselves out of work and deeply in debt. As things turned around over time, many families had to make tough choices about spending, savings, homes, vacations, and so on. In the end, many people found that they were fine with fewer things, and once they cleared debt, they would never return to the burden of it.

We will meet a woman in chapter 9 named Angela Cody-Rouget. Angela founded a company called Major Mom. Her story is a fascinating and inspirational one, and she is a tremendous person. In a nutshell, she had a successful career in the US Air Force and attained the rank of major. After having her second child, however, the demands of a military career started to weigh heavily on her young family, so she resigned her commission and started her company. Major Mom is a professional organizing service. She and her team of organizing experts, whom she calls "liberators," will come to your home or small office and help you get things in order with systems and methods for streamlining your life.

It may sound kind of silly, but Angela uses the term "affluenza" for the affliction so many of us have that requires us to continually acquire more stuff. How many times have you used "retail therapy" as an excuse to blow a hundred dollars at Target or the mall? Do you need those things? Is it worth it if the work you do makes you unhappy? Or are you spending the money to feel better because work makes you unhappy? That might be worse.

Whatever the case, you must decide what changes are required and over what period of time. You might need big changes—finally going back to school to finish a degree you started. Or you might need small changes, such as brushing up a skill set or focusing on your health and wellness. Or maybe you just need to take the leap. What is that old saying? "Stupidity is doing the same thing over and over and expecting a different result." Such is the case with your work life. Sometimes just making the decision to change is the hardest part.

I am not suggesting that you do something rash. Please understand, effective change is planned and properly executed. Do not resolve to change and then go marching in to finally tell your boss what you think of him. No, you want to have a plan, a timeline, and goals associated with it so that you know you are on track.

When I made the decision to leave my corporate job in 2007, I spent months planning the exit. I literally worked up to the last possible day I could to avoid a business trip I did not want to make. I had been put in charge of a new product offering, and I did not believe the product would be successful. I did not want to be publicly associated with it, and there was going to be a trade show in Kentucky where it would be launched early in November of that year. So I worked until

October and then offered extended notice. It worked out fine. I left, and someone else had to cover the product launch. By then I had rented office space, printed business cards, bought computers, and made preparations to move forward without a delay. Of course, there were challenges I could not predict, but the transition was planned and went smoothly.

In my case, I could not have picked a worse time to launch a search firm. The economy was about to run off a cliff, and nobody was going to pay a new recruiting firm full fees at that time. I had to adapt the business many times to find a way to make the money needed to keep going. Talk about getting real. It was tough. But I adapted and made the changes and managed to find work to keep things going for some time. When I finally decided to go back to working for someone else, three years later, it was all my choice once again and based on what I needed to do to be happy and help my family. Change is real. We will come back to that.

Here we are focused on that introspection—the process of understanding who you are and what you plan to become. The women featured here are different from one another. One, Nealene Orinick, is a writer and mom, and the other, Melissa Risteff, is the CEO and cofounder of a new tech start-up. Their demeanors are different, but they have at least one thing in common, and that is that they were wise enough to take stock of their lives in the past couple of years and make some big changes personally and professionally so they could move toward greater satisfaction.

Nealene Orinick

Easily one of the most transformed people I have talked with for this book is a woman I met through my son's school a few years ago named Nealene Orinick. She goes by Neale. When I met her, she was married and raising three boys with her husband, Brian. She was slender and athletic but was coming off a knee injury from a skiing accident.

Neale was one of those people who appeared to have it all and have it all together, yet what I remember about our first meeting was that she seemed to lack confidence and a sense of happiness. She was apologetic about almost everything and followed so many of her comments with disclaimers or qualifying statements. I could not imagine the reason for her insecurity. I did not know then that her marriage was not a happy one anymore, and as a stay-at-home mom married for more than ten years, she was terrified. There was no great drama associated with her marriage; they had just grown apart. For months they lived separately under the same roof, with Neale in the basement guest room. She had no idea what she was going to do to support herself and was feeling enormous guilt about ending the marriage.

Sometimes life teaches us lessons the hard way, and Neale was about to get a jolt. Literally. One day while she was out on a bike ride, a bee flew into her jacket and stung her. As she was riding and trying to take off the jacket, the sleeve got caught on the front tire, and Neale went flying over the handlebars of her bicycle.

She does not remember anything after that, but someone found her standing in the middle of the road, covered in blood. She had literally landed on her face, breaking several facial bones, and if she had not had a helmet on, she would have been killed. She remembers awakening in the hospital and hearing the doctors tell her husband and sister to say their good-byes. Miraculously, however, the injuries did not end her life and, in fact, in some ways helped it begin again. A few days later, she was released from the hospital and went home.

That is when she realized that life is too short and far too precious to waste in an unhappy situation that she had the power to change. She also realized that she owed it to her children, if not to herself, to be happy. Neale was determined to get joy back in her life and to do whatever was necessary to get back on track.

Looking around, she was not sure what she was going to do, but she had always enjoyed writing. She said she was sitting in a coffee shop thinking about it and realizing how many written things there were and how many people must be getting paid to write them, so she put herself out on a couple of freelance websites and became a writer. She laughs about the fact that she helps with a plumbing blog. She never used to know anything about plumbing!

She began writing for others and found it fun and rewarding. Over the past couple of years, she has now built up some regular clients and is editing two community-based magazines. The difference in the woman I interviewed for this book and the woman I met a few years ago is night and day. The most challenging part of her professional development, she told me, was "believing myself worthy of success, not letting feelings of self-doubt and that I was a 'fake'…keep me from pursuing a career as a writer."

Neale has come through this resilient and optimistic. She is now an Ironman triathlete and is training for another race later this year. She also published a fiction book called *The Gifted: Book One* and has begun sequels to it. When I asked her how she mustered the courage to put herself out there as a writer, she said, "I did not know what my potential was until I tried." Neale is an inspiration now. She joked about skiing. She said she loves to ski, especially with her kids, but she is not good at it at all. No matter, she said, "I don't let sucking at things stop me!"

I think Neale is another striking example of a woman who can do anything she wants to do but just needed to push and get a dose of courage to prove it to herself. Once she let herself go, the sky became the limit. I asked her what she would advise her twenty-five-year-old self, and she said, "Be bold, girl! Go after the impossible dream [being a writer]. Failing after going for it, putting it all out there, and coming up short is not as bad as never even trying." Her only regret is that she lacked courage for so long, and she is not sure why that was. Now, she has nowhere to go but up, and she is confident and motivated to see what life brings.

The point of Neale's story, in my view, is that sometimes we do not realize how desperately important it is to find the real you. There are myriad reasons for this problem. From the very beginning, we are told to be ladylike and are given specific parameters within which to operate. Boys are, too, but boys are encouraged more, it seems, to push boundaries and take risks. Many girls are not encouraged in the same way. Too many women settle for what they think they are supposed to want, doing what they think they are supposed to do.

You must take the time to "know thyself," as the Greek sages said. There are many great resources for self-assessments and guidance on this topic. You must think about knowledge, interests, aptitudes, hobbies, skills, values, religion, work ethic, and many other traits that are within you that define what you like to do and how well you may be able to do it. Do not limit the possibilities you explore; be daring in your thinking.

Talk to people who know you well. I once heard that a helpful exercise is to ask a number of people to write down (quickly) the first ten words that come to mind when they think of you. Have them do it extemporaneously so they don't have a lot of time to think about it. Gather those words up and see what you find. Like it or not, that is your personal brand defined by those you know. Congratulations if you love what you see, but if you do not like what you read, you have work to do on yourself.

One of the hardest things in the whole process of getting real and living a real life that is fulfilling and rewarding is that you must, must, must be honest with yourself. Otherwise, there is no point.

Being honest with yourself is difficult. It is especially tricky when it comes to satisfaction with work because we often work hard to get to wherever we are professionally. If, upon arrival, we are not happy, we just settle in and try to pretend we are happy rather than acknowledging that we want to change. This is true in marriage and in our personal lives. And the reason we try to settle is that change itself is hard. Some figure it's easier just to stay where they are than to shift gears, but that is the wrong answer. If you are not happy with your situation, *you are probably the only one who really can change it.* And you owe it to yourself to do so. In the long run, as Neale found, you will be happy that you did.

Melissa Risteff

The process of writing this book continues to offer me surprise after surprise. Not the least of these occurred during an interview I had with a former colleague—actually, a former boss—Melissa Risteff. Melissa is an extraordinary woman and an incredible business talent; she is certainly one of the smartest women with whom I ever worked. I wanted to make sure this book included women of all kinds who have made all types of professional choices. Melissa is one of the most professionally accomplished people in this book.

Melissa completed her undergraduate degree the same year I did, in 1992, and her career has been on a fast-paced trajectory from the beginning. She began at General Electric (GE), where she spent the first several years of her career working in information technology. She was successful immediately, impacting every aspect of the business in a positive way and achieving huge results. She advanced quickly, and by the time she left the company, she had achieved a management position, mentoring and coaching multiple leadership teams.

From GE, she was recruited to Sun Microsystems, where she spent the next six years in a couple of different positions of high visibility, marked by the same rock-star performance. Melissa was enormously successful; as a female in the male-dominated information technology business, she was extraordinary. Her intellect and energy were apparent, and her drive and ambition unwavering.

In 2007, our paths crossed as she came to work at Jones Knowledge, where I also worked. Melissa made an instant impression with everyone. She quickly reined in disparate business endeavors and had people marching to her beat. Deftly managing the $10-million product and marketing budget and redefining product offerings, she was astonishingly effective.

Since her time at Jones, Melissa has taken bigger risks, working for smaller, younger companies than she did early on in her career. She has continued to add to her arsenal of skills and climb corporate ladders. Actively recruited at every turn, Melissa has had her choice of opportunities, and as she has matured, she has gained the respect she deserves for her consistent leadership no matter where she has been.

Recent positions had left Melissa feeling increasingly…well, unfulfilled. She described to me the frustration she was feeling professionally as she noted trends in the roles she had assumed. Too often, she felt, she found herself leading great teams and serving as a buffer between those people and other senior leaders. She found herself straddling those two factions with less and less satisfaction, believing deep down that she could be making a bigger difference. She wondered to herself what that looked like. It took only ninety days and four seminal moments to find out.

Inspiration: In fall 2014, Melissa attended the Denver Women Who Startup event. As Lynn Gangone—now the former dean of the Colorado Women's College at the University of Denver—spoke, something was triggered in her. Lynn was an inspiring force who spoke about previous generations, specifically, her baby-boomer generation, and their failure to bring forward the next generation of women leaders into the field of technology. She challenged the audience to consider how vital it was for them and for all of us to bring young women into technology and into leadership roles in greater numbers. The opportunities exist, but people need guidance and mentoring to capitalize on them.

Melissa walked away from that event thinking that for decades we've been talking about women and equity, pouring money into programs, yet the numbers are in many cases trending in a negative direction. Melissa knew all these things firsthand as an executive in technology for the past fifteen years. She's struggled to build diverse teams and has been an unwavering champion for professional growth. This was her point of inspiration.

Intention: At the time, she was reading a new book by an accomplished coach and friend of hers, Deb Siverson, called *The Cycle of Transformation*. As was the case in so many areas, it seemed the universe was screaming out to her, and she was finding messages all around. In the book, Siverson discusses coaching a client who, instead of having a clear career goal, defaulted to simply climbing the corporate ladder. As with Melissa, his career was a progression of opportunities whereby he never looked for a job and just kept getting tapped on the shoulder.

Siverson wrote, "My client learned the hard way that he was not only on the wrong ladder, it was leaning up against the wrong building." This resonated with

Melissa. Maybe she, too, had the ladder up against the wrong building. This was when she started to clarify her intentions.

Opportunity: Only a month later, Melissa found herself thrust into a near-term transition. As luck would have it, Melissa had a standing dinner planned that very evening with good friend and trusted colleague Laura Farrelly. Melissa brought Laura up to speed on the day's events, and Laura told her how impressed she was with her typical grace under pressure. Laura then simply asked Melissa if she was ready to do something together now. They'd never seriously discussed starting their own business before, but without hesitation, Melissa said yes. It so happened that she had a scheduled vacation with her husband to the Pacific Northwest that Saturday, and they set up a meeting to discuss their next steps upon her return. She remembers it now as one of the best-timed vacations ever. Was she ready to venture out and become an entrepreneur? This was her opportunity.

Courage: In advance of their vacation, they decided to have some spa time. Her husband selected the "Lomilomi" massage, and without much thought, Melissa booked the same for herself. Upon arrival, the specialists started to tell them about the ancient healing practice "conducted with intention." Melissa was looking sideways at Greg, as that was not usually his thing. Nevertheless, in they went. The massage involved ritual and prayer and was an indigenous Polynesian practice. Melissa allowed herself to relax and get into the massage as it progressed. Early in the treatment, among burning sage and chanting, she was asked with enthusiasm, "What spirit animal is with you right now?" Without thought or hesitation, she blurted out, "Raccoon! Raccoon!"

What? Really? She and Greg laughed over it. She and I laughed over it. How absurd! Who thinks of a raccoon as her spirit guide? She recalled feeling foolish for not selecting some more powerful image such as an eagle or lion. When she came out after the treatment, the women at the front desk were saying how amazing it was that she saw a raccoon. And Greg, as she later learned, simply ignored the question and enjoyed his massage.

As it turns out, raccoon is a powerful totem. The raccoon spirit was *exactly right* for Melissa, particularly at that time. When she looked it up, she found that many of the raccoon's traits are formidable: exceedingly adaptive, fierce, resourceful, curious, questioning without fear, clever, and courageous. Then she came upon these riveting quotes and messages from *Earth Magic* by shamanic practitioner, Dr. Steven Farmer:

Raccoon Spirit—You Have Everything You Need

Everything you need you already have. You are complete right now; you are a whole, total person, not an apprentice person on the way to someplace else. Your completeness must be understood by you and experienced in your thoughts as your own personal reality.
—Wayne Dyer

When you cannot distinguish between wants versus needs, or if you can't identify a want as a want, you set yourself up to live in a constant state of craving and disappointment.
—Unknown

If Raccoon has come across your path

You are possibly being asked to let go of a situation, person, belief, or habit. Conversely, it could also mean that you should accept the gifts being offered to you right now by the universe.

Raccoon can also be reminding you to leave no stone unturned in your quest for resolution with the current problem you are facing. Take the time to look at the whole picture—the seen and the unseen to find a solution.

As she told me about this over lunch, she had looked this information up on her phone to share, and she had to hand me the phone to read the quotes; it still chokes her up to realize the message that was being sent to her at that time. Sometimes, it seems, the universe really does send us what we need if we are aware enough to see it. Timing was everything in this story. This was when she gained her courage.

Melissa told me that she came to the idea slowly, realizing that she had been told quite directly by recruiters and others that she should start her own business and that she was destined to be a CEO. She had at times felt like an apprentice in a constant state of craving. Could she be ready? Did she really have the experience she needed? She continued to be courted for leadership roles with other technology companies, and she continued to turn them down. Each time it got easier.

"Being wanted is success," she asked me, "right?" Well, maybe for some, but in her heart or gut, she knew it was time. It took the right inspiration, clarity around her intentions, the opportunity, and courage.

So was born the company that she and her business partner, Laura Farrelly, have founded, Couragion. Couragion's mission is to inspire young people to pursue careers in science, technology, engineering, and math (STEM). Just four months after incorporation, they launched a career and self-discovery application and signed their first two agreements with schools. As cofounder and CEO, Melissa is squarely in her ideal professional situation. She is creating technology to provide role models for the next generation of leaders. She has found what she was looking for by creating it herself.

The Melissa I met with for this book is light years away from the Melissa I knew in 2007. This Melissa is at peace in her skin and is radiant with confidence and optimism. She is calmer and more self-assured while simultaneously being less assertive, or at least not edgy. This Melissa knows exactly what she wants *for herself* and does not appear to be trying to prove anything or to win anyone over. She is settled. It is an amazing difference in such a short time, and it makes me so happy for her.

I don't think I ever talked about Melissa much before. I thought of her as an ambitious, smart woman who was marching her way to the forefront. Now I see her as an accomplished, confident woman with an even stride and a happier spirit. I realize few who read this book are on the path she was on, and, of course, as I have said before, entrepreneurism is not for everyone—certainly not tech entrepreneurism. The lesson in Melissa's story, as I see it, is one of authenticity.

From where I am standing, I see now that Melissa does not have to put on a persona regarding her work and who she is. Her work is clearly part of her, because she is doing something that matters to her and for her. That is a huge accomplishment. Further, she has finally realized what motivates and rewards her by following her own vision of herself and staying true to her inner voice. I know it sounds touchy-feely, but gut instincts sometimes are.

When there is a message out there for you, often it does not come as directly as the raccoon spirit in the Lomilomi massage. The spirit most often just whispers to us softly. It is up to us to turn down the white noise and listen for that voice. Then it is up to each of us to decide how to move forward, at what pace, in what direction, and with what goals in mind.

The old saying about a journey of a thousand steps beginning with one step is true. Transformation of personal life and career and inner self do not occur in one fell swoop but rather when we iterate on our goals and on ourselves, constantly refining the vision and shaping ourselves for the next version of success we are to realize. It's an exercise in self-awareness, faith, and discipline. And, as I have stated before, often a single moment of certainty never really appears. Often we follow our instinct to realize our best selves. However, marching down the right path is a strangely calming thing, even in the face of risk or doubt. It's kind of like driving down the road once you have had your tires checked, filled, balanced, and aligned. The car works the same way, but it feels smoother or somehow more comfortable. It's a subtle difference, but one you can feel.

This is one of the great areas in which I hope to inspire readers. You must believe in a version of yourself that has you happy, well, doing work you love, and feeling in sync with your life. That is not to say life will be perfect all the time. Of course it will not be, but when you take the bold steps and move toward the version of yourself that is more authentic, you will find the strength of spirit and the energy to handle the bumps better. It is a wonderful, intangible feeling, and I wish it for each of you. Take the time to find out what makes your heart sing.

Here are some questions to ask yourself and to answer honestly. Write the answers down. Mull them over. Consider every possibility, no matter how large or difficult it seems. Do not spend time initially on any of the "why I can't" responses but focus on the "what if I could" instead. I am completely serious. You have to start asking yourself these questions if you are going to start to change anything.

And if you don't know what you need to change to be happier or more satisfied, this is the beginning of that discovery process.

Look at these answers, once you have them, and compare them to a related list that describes what you are doing now to see how far apart they are. Maybe small changes over time are all it will take. Or maybe you have to hunker down, start some serious planning, and make big decisions and big changes.

The point is, you must start somewhere, and you must believe that the change is possible and that you deserve to have the best life you can have. There is an old quote I love. I do not know whom to credit, but it says, "What you have is your gift from God. What you do with it is your gift back to him." Whether you believe in God or not, hopefully you understand what I am saying. You have the potential to do many things, and you have desires that will make those things feel good and true. You have to align the two, and when you do, you will be on the best path for yourself that there is. Keep in mind, *you are the only one who has the answers.* The good news is, you do have them within you already; you just need to find them, and you can absolutely do that!

Start with these questions:

- What makes you smile?
- What excites you?
- What do you love doing?
- What are you good at?
- What is your single greatest strength?
- What would you do if money were no object?
- What would you do if you knew you could not fail? (Not original but a great question I have asked myself many times!)
- What do you want to accomplish in your life at some point? Are you on the path to accomplishing those things?
- As a young person, did you have goals that you have given up on? Is there value in reexamining those?
- How do you want to be remembered?

All kinds of resources are available to you for self-evaluation. You may want to look into some of them. But I believe that no matter what those tests or experts say, if you have not done this soul searching and really thought about what makes you tick, you will not come to the best conclusion. Keep in mind that you do not have to share this information with anyone. But you have to at least be able to *open up to yourself.* There is no hope of authentic happiness if you cannot be honest with yourself. I believe that is one of the most important takeaways from this book and an indisputable fact. Self-honesty is tough. It is really tough, but it is the place from which every success must emanate.

CHAPTER 4

Your Real Options

Knowing what you want is the first step toward getting it.
—Mae West

One of the most striking things as I talked to the women for this book and what I want to emphasize to readers is the power of *believing in a possibility*. So often, over the years, I have spoken to women either personally or in professional settings who have not believed they could change their lives. For whatever reason, an abundance of women truly believe that they are stuck in their current situation and that it will not change. What they either refuse to see or refuse to acknowledge is that the power to change lies within all of us. It truly does. But it requires a few key things:

- The belief that change is truly possible
- The ability to create a plan that is actionable and realistic
- The willingness to take some risk
- The resilience to bounce back from challenges
- The tenacity to keep bouncing back and keep adjusting
- The patience to move as slowly as needed
- The determination to move quickly when needed
- The confidence in yourself to visualize the goal
- The forgiveness for yourself when you make mistakes or stumble
- The presence of mind to recognize and celebrate milestones

Believing that change is possible is the first step. Sounds simple, but if you do not believe you can do what you set forth to do, then there is no point in trying, as I believe you will inevitably fail. Surely you have heard Henry Ford's famous quote: "Whether you believe you can or you believe you cannot, you are right." To say attitude is everything sounds cliché, but it is an important element in the process of change. Whether it is a major career change, going back to school, finding a new job, dieting, or whatever the change is, *you must be able to visualize what that success looks like for you.* That vision is literally the goal you have to keep in front of you at all times.

There are lots of ways to do this, if you are not simply able to hold an image in your heart and mind. Some people literally find photos or other visual reminders and surround themselves with them. Some people journal as a means to keep focusing on the goal. Some meditate, exercise, or find other activities that they enjoy to help them zone in on their goals. It is a process of mental discipline that helps you keep the goal real, which requires some practice and determination.

When I decided that I wanted to exit my corporate job, for example, and launch DeCoste & Associates, it took me a long time to be able to picture myself doing it. Literally, I had to picture myself offering a letter of resignation, packing my boxes, saying good-bye to colleagues and friends, and then going to work for myself. But I clearly remember the day I decided I was going to do it.

We had just gotten paid. For some reason I was looking at a paycheck (not sure why it was not a direct deposit, as I think about it). In the office/cubicle next to me, a colleague who had been with the company for years longer than I had been was complaining about the fact that the owner, who was wealthy, had put a freeze on bonuses five years earlier and few people (if any) had even gotten cost-of-living increases in quite some time. She was going on and on about what a tightwad he was.

As I sat and listened to her and stared at his signature on my paycheck, I started to wonder if I could ever be either brave or stupid enough to try to work for myself. It was like a scene in a movie, where all of a sudden, my focus went elsewhere, and I could not hear my neighbor's complaining anymore. All I could envision was what life would be like if I could work on my own terms.

It seemed outrageous. My job was solid and not difficult, and I worked four miles from home. I had even negotiated a four-day workweek by the time I left. I had benefits, three weeks of vacation time, 100 percent tuition reimbursement, a nice office, and great friends there, yet all I wanted was to be on my own. At that time, my son was around eighteen months old. I decided, after talking to my husband, that my goal was to be free of that job, by my own choice, by the time our son entered kindergarten.

Suddenly everything changed. I vowed I would never again work for someone else; that signature would be the last one other than my own that I would see on a paycheck, hopefully for the rest of my life. Once I made up my mind, even with a nearly three-year runway in front of me, everything felt better. The prospect of being out on my own took the weight of the world off my shoulders, it seemed. I had a new clarity of purpose that motivated me in entirely different ways.

The transition was not easy. I remember every step of that journey, and I was terrified that I was making a mistake. But by the time I was actually doing it, the goal had become so big and so real for me that there simply was no going back. Those last days before I gave notice were incredibly difficult. Sitting in a car in the parking garage, I had to give myself pep talks every morning to go into the office, work, keep my head down, and just get through to the day when I could give notice. I literally worked until the last possible day before I handed in my resignation—with an image in my head of what it would be like to drive to my new office on the other side of town. For me, having that office was important, too, as a symbol that the new job was real. I would not have been as comfortable working from home initially; having the office to go to was important to me, but that was a big financial decision I made also to ensure my dedication. I had to start making money right away because I was paying office rent.

We will talk about strategy a bit later, so I am not going to drill down on the planning part here. However, it must be noted that to achieve a big change, you must have a plan. I believe this firmly. It is true that some people are impetuous and can fly by the seat of their pants, but I do not believe that for most of us spontaneity is great when it comes to life-changing career and personal decisions.

For one thing, you have to think through all the steps—and I mean *all* of them. You have to envision yourself actually taking every one of those steps over and over in your mind. You want to be sure you have not underestimated the time, resources, or talent required to do whatever it is you think you will be doing. It is especially helpful to have a mentor or role model you can talk to who has been down the path before. I did not, but I had worked for many people in the recruiting industry who started on their own, and I knew what that looked and felt like from their perspectives.

One of the biggest factors in understanding your real options comes down to one little word: *risk*. It sounds simple enough, but you must do some real soul searching to determine how much risk you are willing to take. If you are married or in a long-term relationship and if you have children or other family to support, this is a big, big question. If you are not willing to take any chances, if risk is something you have no tolerance for, well, then it is difficult to make a change. It's that simple. Nothing ventured, nothing gained. I could offer you a million quotes and clichés, but the bottom line is that change requires risk.

It is extremely helpful to have serious conversations about this topic with yourself and with anyone else who has a say in the matter. For example, my husband and I talked a lot about this when I launched the company. His support is what made it possible for me to leave my job; however, we had to rework our budget to account for the loss of 50 percent of our household income and factor in all the foreseeable expenses for a while, so we fully understood what we were getting into. You cannot skip this step.

We literally went line by line through the budget to see where we would have cuts and where there would be increases in spending to account for the launch of the business. We had to talk about household budgeting, vacations, college and retirement savings, and more.

When it came down to it, however, there was one risk we agreed we would not take, and that was drawing any money from our home's equity. We agreed that we would be able to risk the cuts and the cutbacks, but never would we risk the house. That felt fair to me and safe for my husband, and, thankfully, it worked. We did not ever have to leverage our house, though we did take many other risks to keep things moving along.

There is also something to be said for resiliency and bouncing back from mistakes. The road to change is not an easy one; there will be setbacks and frustration, and you will make mistakes. Hopefully, if you plan carefully enough and are sincerely honest with yourself, you will have less to worry about than some, but just know that there will be challenges. What is that old saying? "If it were easy, everyone would do it." Nothing could be truer.

When we started the business, I knew that I would have a hard time simultaneously costing us money and not contributing income to the family. I am a financial worrier and always have been. I love making money, but I do not like to manage it. We had always had a good system: my husband was happy to manage the financials, and I was happy to contribute. That said, when it was clear that I would not be contributing, initially at least, I had to stay accountable without fretting over money every day. It was a big challenge. *I needed to find a way to stay motivated and positive even without validation from a regular paycheck.* Having worked consistently in my life since I lied about my age to get my first job, I defined myself and measured my success, at least to some degree, by that paycheck.

I was super-motivated and wanted everything to happen *now*. Patience is not one of my strengths, to say the least, so I had to work hard to define milestones so that I could feel myself actually meeting measurable goals. Sometimes those goals may not seem important, but when you have big goals that require considerable amounts of time or resources, you have to look at things with a fresh perspective.

I remember when I first got out of college and was trying to figure out what to do professionally with my BA in language studies. I didn't have a career plan going in but assumed that fluency in foreign languages would be helpful, and since not everyone could do them, German and Spanish seemed a better bet than history or philosophy. As I said, I had worked as a teenager and knew that I was good with people and could sell, but I really did not know where to start. It was my dad who said to me, "Just make a choice. Pick a job you think you might like and that you think you might be good at, and then give it six months of your best effort before you try to evaluate it because *the moment of absolute certainty may never come.*" That advice has stuck with me throughout my life. The moment of absolute certainty may never come, but you have to give it a try and give it some time.

This is true when you are making life and career changes as well. So when we agreed that I would start the business, we used the same logic. I was to fling myself into it wholeheartedly and without regret or fear and without looking over my shoulder. However, I also agreed to sit down with my husband, Paul, every six months and "look at a spreadsheet," as he put it. We agreed to that level of accountability so that I would have a true perspective of what I was bringing in, what was going out, and what the net was. It worked for us.

Maybe you need a similar plan or something entirely different. My point is, however, that you must figure out a way to adjust your pace to the circumstances. Sometimes you will have to charge at your goals with all the force you can muster; conversely, sometimes—and this is harder for many—*sometimes, you have to be incredibly patient and allow events to unfold at their own pace.* There are, of course, many factors you cannot control no matter how much you may want to. When you are talking about your career and big life choices, you still have to relinquish a little bit of control to forces greater than or outside of yourself.

One of my favorite quotes—among the many I have collected, and one of the first quotes I ever taught my son—is one by Vince Lombardi: "Winners never quit and quitters never win."

Yes, "Winners never quit and quitters never win." I have quit things in my life. I have resigned from jobs. I never did master Tai Chi. I have quit smoking, twice. But in general, I do not like quitting or giving up. I am a relentless person. This is true of all of the amazing women I interviewed in this book. They are not quitters. None of them are.

Tenacity is required when you are facing big goals, and setbacks—something we will talk more about throughout the book—are inevitable. But please know that even when you face a roadblock or a challenge, optimism will go a long, long way. You may have to adjust the plan; many women we will talk about here have adjusted, as have I, but you cannot give up on the dream. Go back to whatever you are using to keep yourself motivated, and drink it in. You have to keep moving forward.

Here in chapter 4, we are looking at two stories that involve options and choices. One of these is a clear-cut story and a good example of a choice many of us face at some point when looking at career and family. Vickie Thomas tells us about the fork in the road that she faced after achieving big goals in one arena and having to decide which path was the right one for her. Not an easy choice and certainly life changing, but she made her decision and moved forward, and she has no regrets.

The other story is more transformational than binary. Susie Wargin's career transformation is a success story that shows us that even someone in a high-profile and public career can navigate change over time by taking all the necessary steps slowly and steadily and by being strategic. Both show, though, that we are faced with choices, and we have to be realistic about options and the pathway from point A to point B. Finding success sometimes requires incremental steps.

Finally, along these lines, try to find ways to celebrate little successes. If you can, identify them in advance. For example, how many times have you been in a shop and seen a dollar framed? I have a dollar on my desk, still in the envelope it was sent in, from the first check I cashed that was made out to the company. I remember that day as clearly as if it were yesterday. I remember my first placement, over twenty years ago, as a recruiter. I remember his name and the client.

Try to identify steps or stages that will constitute the path to success. It is vital that you do this because, as so many women have affirmed, it is often difficult to recognize success in increments. It's crucial and exceedingly helpful when you can find ways to reassure yourself that you have chosen the right path, that you are on it, and that you are truly heading in the direction of your dreams. Doing so will put wind in your sails.

Vickie Thomas

This is a short story compared to some of the others, but I could not resist including it, because it made me smile and is 100 percent true. Vickie Thomas is the founder of the Thomas Group, a successful branding and marketing strategy company that she has owned for many years. I met Vickie at a women's conference put on by our chamber of commerce in South Metro Denver back in 2009. She had been an active chamber leader and was a speaker at the conference. I remember her clearly because she had a large presence and was a central figure. She stood out to me as I realized she was doing what I wanted to be doing: leading conferences, writing, and speaking. I was curious about her and her path.

As life would have it, though, shortly after that conference, she decided to move in another direction. After nearly twenty years helping to build the chamber, she wanted to focus her attention elsewhere, and she slipped off my radar. Her name came up once in a while, but I lost track of her.

Fast-forward, however, to fall 2014, and the same women's group at the chamber was holding its annual kickoff meeting. I had decided to become part of the leadership team (in part for preparation of this book), and at the event, I bumped into Vickie again. I was astonished at her transformation! She must have dropped fifty pounds. Maybe more. She looked to be less than half of her old size. I have never personally seen someone go through such a radical change in size. She looked amazing. She also looked relaxed and happy, and I was delighted to chat with her and to have her agree that I could follow up for a meeting.

As I mentioned, the initial reason she had been of interest was that I was curious about her path to success and any advice she might offer me as I tried to follow a similar route. Working on this book was also a great excuse, because she'd had success as a writer and would certainly have some opinions and perhaps more advice. Not knowing her well, I was not sure if she would want to be featured in the book, so I did not want to seem too pushy. Thankfully, she was incredibly gracious and offered her full support.

In the context of getting to know her background, she shared a bit of her personal story that clearly falls into the category of choices, and I cannot resist sharing it. When Vickie was young, she had the chance to accompany her former husband to Saudi Arabia, the first international move for both of them. She worked there for five years, enjoying the experience immensely, and it tuned her in to global business. Eventually, both the marriage and the job came to an end.

As she was planning her future on the way back to the United States, she decided a corporate career would be her best option, and she resolved—on the plane as she returned to the United States—that her goal was to become vice president of a large company, which was still fairly rare for a female at that time. Why, I asked, vice president? Vickie laughed, reflecting on that long-ago moment, and said she was not sure why, but that was what she thought her future and her success would look like, and that was what she wanted.

So Vickie secured a position with PepsiCo and began to climb the ladder. She threw herself headlong into her work, was a devoted employee and leader, and enjoyed great success and happiness. As fortune would have it, though, she faced a choice. She met a charming man around this time who lived in California. He had a young son whom he and his wife had recently adopted. Sadly, his wife had passed away suddenly and unexpectedly, and he and his son, Jason, were still mourning the loss. However, life took an unexpected turn as the newfound friendship evolved, and Richard and Vickie fell in love.

Vickie's job allowed for quite a bit of travel but was still based at a PepsiCo subsidiary office in Washington, DC. When Richard's proposal came, as fate would have it, so did the offer of a promotion. You may have guessed—a vice presidency, and the first one in that division ever offered to a woman. When she told me the story with a smile, remembering that moment, she said she thought about the job, and then she thought about her feelings for Richard. Then she thought about the sweet little boy who was around three years old at the time. He'd been put up for adoption, and then he lost his new mom. She was torn, but it was not really that hard to decide in the end. She chose the boys. And she has never regretted it.

Laughing, she said she consoled herself by "getting my own business cards that said 'president' in the title." She added, "You know what that means? Not much really!"

Nonetheless, she started her own small consulting practice in branding and marketing. Mostly, in the early days, she worked part-time and focused on her family, raising Jason and being happy with the choice she had made. As it turned out, children were not possible for them, so the fact that they had him was even more special.

Sometimes the work choices we make put work in the backseat. That is fine. We will talk about this over and over throughout the book, but the definition of success for one woman will be different than it is for another. Vickie has built a great life for herself. Once her son was in school, she refocused on work and built up a profitable book of business that kept her busy. Now she can choose when and how much she works. She can arrange work to accommodate her life, traveling to clients in cities around the country where she has family or when her husband is traveling. It has worked out well, and she has no regrets.

Not all of us will face such a stark decision, but through Vickie's story, we see that things find a way to work themselves out when we follow our instincts and let life lead us down unexpected paths.

Susie Wargin

Not too many of us can say that Peyton Manning and the Denver Broncos were instrumental in helping us make career choices, but Susie Wargin can. Susie is another extraordinary woman I came to know through my son's school PTO, and her story of career development and then radical change is one of the most striking I have ever heard. Also, because Susie works in the media, her story has not been as private as some, so she has the added pressure of dealing with the changes in a public setting.

Susie has been well-known here in Denver for over twenty years as a sports anchor for KUSA-TV (9News/NBC affiliate) and for 850KOA Radio. She is well liked in both roles.

Susie's career has been one of gradual ascension after college; she moved from DJ work to radio and then to TV. She has charted a path in a field where not many women achieve the highest levels of success, and then she chose to make a change and reprioritize, which ultimately meant an entire career transformation in her forties.

Susie is married and has two great kids, and her family is an important part of the story also. It was the classic case of knowing that if family was to remain a priority, then work had to change. In the TV news business, typically, there are not many choices, and, because of the contractual nature of the work, there is not much flexibility. Admittedly, too, many argue that the position Susie had as a sports anchor on the number-one TV station in town is just the kind of job nobody chooses to leave. But she did.

In March 2012, her college alma mater, Colorado State University (CSU), made it into the NCAA basketball tournament, and 9News asked Susie to go to Louisville, Kentucky, to cover the first, and potentially second, round of CSU's games. As one of the few anchors who could be a one-man/woman band, she knew how to write, plan, shoot, and submit the story alone, so she did not have a crew traveling with her.

The Rams lost in the first round of the tournament, so Susie did a live recap of the game for the ten o'clock evening news and was scheduled to return to Denver the next day. To be on the news in Denver at 10:20 p.m. meant that she was still up at 12:30 a.m. EST for the live shot. After her live shot, she grabbed about three hours of sleep and then headed to the airport to return her rental car and board a 6:00 a.m. flight. After the three-and-a-half-hour flight home, Susie planned to drive straight from Denver International Airport to her daughter's dance competition.

Upon landing in Denver, Susie did what everyone does: turned on her phone. It was piled up with voice messages and texts, including a few from her sports director who told her the station had tracked the jet of Bronco's owner, Pat Bowlen, to North Carolina. They suspected Broncos' general manager, John Elway, and head coach, John Fox, were watching Peyton Manning throw at Duke University. Susie was told she was booked on a flight to Raleigh and needed to find them to capture a story and submit it as quickly as possible. When she questioned the plan about returning to the East Coast after just having been there (and not wanting to disappoint her daughter), she was told, "Sorry. We are in the business of breaking news."

So she called her husband to tell him the plan. Her husband called the general manager of the station, with whom he was acquainted, and tried to explain about the dance competition and the logic of trying to find Peyton somewhere on the Duke campus. But he, too, was told that was the nature of the business. Susie sat in her car and cried as she got ready to call her daughter and break the bad news. Just before she was to head back into the airport, her sports director called and told her never mind. The meeting at Duke had been fast, and Bowlen's plane was getting ready to take off. Heartbreak was averted for her daughter; however, Susie decided right then that she needed to plan a change and start exploring other options.

She had just recently signed a new contract and was only six months into a three-year commitment. So she had two and one-half years to figure out a career change, but she did not know what she would do. She considered her roles in many charitable bike rides and some of the community-based work she had done. She considered the event industry as an option. She wanted something fun and different that offered some autonomy and flexibility as well. She continued to quietly explore options over the next few months.

Susie had a long-standing habit of having lunch with her mom every January to celebrate her mom's birthday. The two were close and had followed similar work paths: succeeding in a male-dominated industry. Susie's mom made her way into the real estate business in the mid-1970s when few women worked in the industry. She was one of the first women "allowed" into RE/MAX. Every year, her mom would ask her to consider real estate.

At their lunch meeting in January 2013, her mom asked again, and this time Susie said, "Okay." She had been thinking about it, and the move made perfect sense to her. She had her mom—who had great connections—as a resource and mentor, and this was a career she could enter on a planned schedule while maintaining some autonomy.

So she went to real estate school on the side, without letting on at 9News. She continued to work as a morning sports anchor, getting up at 1:30 a.m. to be at the station by 3:00 a.m. and on the air for the 5:00 a.m. news. When her shift ended, she would head to real estate school in the afternoons. In June 2013, she got her real estate license. She was thrilled! She had her first listing by November 2013.

Word eventually got around about her changes. Typically six months before a contract ends, management will call in anchors and reporters to talk about what's next. If they want to keep the talent, they will have an envelope with a new contract ready to go at that meeting. When Susie was called in six months prior to her contract ending, there was no envelope.

Her general manager said, "A little bird told me you got your real estate license." Susie concurred and said she didn't plan to renew her contract because she wanted to sell real estate full-time. The freedom, relationships, and monetary benefits were already blossoming. 9News asked if she would still freelance exclusively for them and continue to leave the door open for fill-in work and special projects. It worked out perfectly.

In the meantime, a local radio station heard she was leaving 9News and approached her about full-time work in spring 2014. She turned it down, saying she had left full-time work to pursue more flexibility and family time. The station came back again with a sweeter offer: the chance to do a show with Dave Logan, longtime friend and Denver sports icon, that would air from 3:00 to 5:00 p.m. Monday through Friday—along with a salary and insurance benefits. It was as if the universe was smiling on her and giving her a bit of everything she wanted as she launched her new career.

Susie is off to the races with her real estate business now. Last year she had nine deals total. As of the writing of this story in May 2015, she had thirteen completed on the books. She tends to work mostly with friends, friends of friends, and their referrals. She loves it and is home more often with her family.

For Susie, this was just the right mix of strategy and luck, but that has been the case her whole career, she said. She has always believed in preparedness as a secret to success and said one of her favorite quotes came from former Broncos wide receiver Rod Smith: "Opportunity is when luck meets preparation." In her life and in her work, Susie strives to be abundantly prepared, and she does not believe in excuses.

Asked about succeeding as a sports journalist with so many men in the field, Susie said she never felt gender was an obstacle. In fact, she said, it was an advantage. Being different, she said, is good, but you have to "know your stuff; treat people like people and with respect." She added, "And don't be a bitch!" Susie believes that karma really stinks if you treat people poorly. She always tried to show that she cared about the people behind the story and not just about the story. As a woman, she said, it was more natural to ask about how a player's wife and kids were doing than it would be for a man. Many had seen her work through two pregnancies, so they knew she had that role as well and were respectful. Above all else, she said, she does not believe in having a persona. She likes to be herself, and that has served her well.

Though she did make the change of careers for her family, she is not delusional about a mythical work-life balance. She agrees that no such thing exists. She calls it a "work-life blend." She tries to involve her family in her work and to have it all coexist. She said she likes to think of it as "harmonizing," a term her priest used in a sermon once that stuck with her. Her kids know that is one of her buzzwords.

What is success for her now? It is all of this. Her life is a success. On top of her career change, her husband, Mike, went through some serious health issues. He discovered that he had a brain tumor (benign), and they battled through that together. Once he was on the well side again, he decided he wanted a change. He had been a private school administrator, but life is too short to do something that is no longer fulfilling. So he turned to a trade he loves, crafting handmade goods and—of all things—a career as a poker player!

Susie is matter-of-fact and positive about everything in her life. She is a driven person but not to the extent that she won't sit and smell the roses. When I was interviewing her for this book, she came down to her office fresh from a shower with wet hair and no makeup. Her house was inside out; they were replacing floors and cabinets. Her kitchen was set up in the garage, and she told me they had eaten dinner the night before on the floor, picnic style—and loved it!

She is a goal setter but admits she does not really focus on that. She tries to take things one step at a time, trying to keep it real, not make mistakes, stay on top of things, and be trustworthy. She has a list for everything and manages her home and her business with multiple planners, calendars, and spreadsheets. She laughs about all of the lists.

Priorities change, but she admits that there is not time to do everything; you have to allow yourself flexibility. We talked about the importance, for example, of networking. Yes, she conceded, it is extremely important, but "you have to do smart networking." You have to "pick the right events and the right people. People who can help you but also people you can help. Look for your tribes," she said, "the people you have things in common with, and always, always be asking what you can do for them first." Also, she added, "Loyalty matters."

If she could give her twenty-five-year-old self advice, what would it be? Be patient. Keep your options open. Always follow up. (She almost missed out on her first job by not following up. When she was discouraged that she had not heard back after she submitted a demo tape, her then boyfriend (now husband) told her to call and make sure they had received it. She did. They had not. She resent it. She got the job.)

What inspires her? People do. She likes to make people happy. She likes to be liked, and she likes to be positive. She kept coming back to luck and preparation. "You have to be ready when opportunity comes your way," she said, and you have to be "a little bit fearless sometimes." She added, "Trust yourself. You will figure it out." Plus, she said, "We all have to learn how to fail."

My favorite part of our conversation came back to where I began with this book. Susie said, "When you want something, you have to put it out in the universe and then be ready." Smiling, she added, "If you feel stuck, you will be stuck. Look around and make the tentacles connect. Ask yourself, 'What do I need to do?' Then go do that. Just go do it."

CHAPTER 5

Real Strategy

Optimism is a strategy for making a better future. Because
unless you believe that the future can be better, you are
unlikely to step up and take responsibility for making it so.
—Noam Chomsky

As I have said before, the process of writing this book has taught me several lessons. The one I still struggle to convey correctly is what this chapter is all about: career change and strategy. I will say that Kimberly Alexander is the right person for me to feature here. Kimberly's book, *The Results Map*, aligns with what I believe the strategy should look like. I have written curricula on this subject several times, and there is a general methodology to making big changes strategically.

For starters, a bit of introspection is required when you must take stock of where you are. Then there are processes of different types to cull options, align goals, and consider timeline benchmarks. This is universally known, and I believe it is a true and proven approach.

What I have learned through the writing of this book, however, is that it is not always quite so tidy or prescriptive. Real strategy and planning for real change—for women, in particular—requires a level of elasticity that I had not thought of before. The women in this book and others I have spoken with admit that they planned to some extent but not quite in a bulleted list with permanent marker.

In other words, planning for change requires a tolerance for the unexpected, and strategizing for change requires building the unexpected into the plan.

Real strategy means resiliency for women. Real strategy looks ahead and takes aim but allows for bounce back and correction at all times. This is partly because so many women have multiple responsibilities that they have to allow for; in addition, the stars do not always align, or stay aligned, as we hope. For example, if the demand of family changes, we most often adjust to suit that need. This is not to say that men don't also deal with these challenges, but I think it's fair to say that, in most cases (maybe less than it used to be, but still most), if there is a challenge at home and someone has to adjust professionally—whatever that means—most often it is the woman who makes the change to cover the situation. Perhaps it is because she is the better person to meet the need at home; perhaps she earns less, so it is purely a practical choice. Whatever the reason, we get derailed from our goals and plans more easily.

Real strategy takes this fact into consideration. Changes cannot always take place on a firm timeline. That is where tenacity comes into play. Also, this is where the importance of a supportive network is critical. Kimberly refers to it in her book as "your crew." We all need a support network. That is why the chapter topics of strategy and networking are next to each other in this book—because I think they are inextricably tied.

As I interviewed for this book, I heard time and again the importance of having friends or of going and finding some good friends. We cannot do everything alone, though we often feel as if it's easier that way. We need the support that friends offer, and we can find great strength just in sharing our stories. That is part of a real strategy also.

If you are serious about changing something in your life, you have to be willing and able to articulate it to others. You have to put it out there, and you have to own it. Being accountable for goals is the best way to stick to them and is an easy way to take a plan and make it a strategy. Perhaps you've heard about SMART goals, a term most often attributed to Peter Drucker? The *T*, which stands for time lined, is sometimes the hardest part because of all the balls you may be juggling.

But with the right support, the right "crew," as Kimberly would say, you will have people there to help you stay on track when you deviate; they will remind you why you chose the course in the first place.

Kimberly Alexander

If I were to add a chapter to the book, it might be titled Real Results because of the next woman. Kimberly Alexander is a speaker, trainer, and author of the book *The Results Map*, and she is one of the reasons I decided to take on this project in the first place. I will pause here with an aside that I have not mentioned before: one thing I strongly believe is that people are brought into our lives for a reason. It is often one of my great challenges and joys to try to figure out that reason. I think it is really an entirely separate exercise to take stock of the people around me and see if I can uncover how there can be mutual benefit in working together or getting to know them.

Such was definitely the case with Kimberly. She and I are both members of the South Metro Denver Chamber of Commerce. I have been a member since 2008, and Kimberly came into the chamber in 2010, when I was around but less involved. Suddenly I was hearing about her from people I kept running into. Many people asked if I knew her and told me we had to meet. We finally did meet at a leadership retreat in 2012; however, we did not really connect until just a few months ago when I got back into the Women in Business group at the chamber.

While I was on a bit of a hiatus from the chamber, she was climbing the ladder, publishing her own first book and building her brand. She is on the executive board for several committees, including Health and Wellness and Women in Business, and is on the chamber's board of directors. Kimberly is well known, greatly appreciated, and wildly respected among chamber members of all levels and within the greater business community. Her dedication to work, excellent attitude, and easy demeanor have ingratiated her to everyone who knows her, and her book has inspired many more.

Kimberly and I are like-minded in many areas, and there are also some commonalities in our life stories. Like me, Kimberly is from Orange County, California. She said she had a very ordinary upbringing but always knew she was extraordinarily ambitious. That proved to be true. After finishing a two-year college program in fashion, Kimberly went to work in one of the largest department stores in southern California, Robinsons-May, and she began her rocket-shot to the top with Estee Lauder. By age twenty-two, she had more responsibility than most of us imagine at that time, working regionally for

Lauder in San Diego and Orange County. Her boss once told her after a promotion, "If I had known how young you were, there is no way I would have given you this job!" But she got it, and she was successful in the traditional sense of the word.

As she retells the story, she just remembers getting the stuff she'd always wanted. Big brick cell phone. Check. Jeep Cherokee. Check. Beautiful clothes. Check. It was all the stuff she'd dreamed of as a girl, and it made her feel successful.

Eventually, she was transferred to Colorado, but there was a mix-up, and, in the end, she found herself needing a new job. So she went to work for Bausch and Lomb. The same process repeated itself. She was an all-star performer in the sunglasses industry. She had fun. She traveled. She kept getting stuff, and she thought life was good.

As is often the case, though, there were some bumps in the road. She had married, and that was not going well, so it ended quickly and easily. Her job changed again, and she found herself in the travel industry—also working at a hotel, mostly for the associated travel benefits. She was on her own briefly until she met her husband, J. J., who is an entrepreneur.

With his encouragement, she went a somewhat different direction and got back into cosmetics but in a major network-marketing firm. (If you are not familiar with that term, it refers to companies such as Tupperware or Amway, in which you build a team and sell directly on your own.) This time, she really hit the fast track. Within a short period, she was once again a multimillion-dollar producer with many people beneath her on the chain. She was happy and felt as if she was making a difference helping others build their businesses, making money herself, and getting back on the fast track to business success.

During this time, she also had two children with J. J. He had started his own businesses as a franchisee and was doing well. The girls were small, and Kimberly was on the fast track. At this point of her story, however, the momentum in her voice changed, and I realized she was going to need a tissue. Kimberly was working herself to death. She was so obsessed with business success that she lost sight of many important things, and she said, "I hurt people."

Sometimes she'd be packing for trips she had forgotten to tell J. J. were scheduled. When she was on the road, she missed lots of milestones, including birthdays, sometimes forgetting even to call her girls. She was completely out of balance and did not even realize her family was desperate to have her back until, in tears, her husband broke down and begged her, "Please come back to us." She had been going so fast and so furiously that she had not noticed how much she was missed. It had gone too far.

She also acknowledged that she did not feel at all well. She had not been looking in the mirror, literally and figuratively. I guess working in cosmetics has advantages, but Kimberly said she looked and felt like a train wreck. Her dietary habits were terrible. She leaned on wine too heavily, she thought, but it was all part of the grind.

Then another roadblock appeared in the form of the type of boss we all dread. She worked for a woman who was known to do *whatever* it took to move up the ladder, and as Kimberly edged closer to the upper echelons of the company in New York, the boss was feeling threatened. In the long run, the writing was on the wall. Kimberly knew it was time to plan her exit, so she began to do just that.

Her book, *The Results Map*, was born out of that process. The book captures the exact way in which Kimberly took inventory of her own situation, determined the limitations and prospects that lay before her, rallied the right support network around her, and set forth to change with specific goals in mind. As she created and documented the process and used it to make changes herself, she recognized others might also benefit.

She went on to another company with a similar network sales approach and was successful again, of course, but this time more intentionally so. This company was a wellness company, too, so she was able to take advantage of access to products that helped her get healthier, stronger, and more in balance physically.

Kimberly enjoyed that company and was at the top of her game when the founder invited her to an exclusive leadership retreat in Sundance, Utah, for the star sales performers. At that retreat, given the time to really reflect on where she had been and what she was doing now, Kimberly realized it was time "to leave and to spread my wings." She had a great mentor in that position, someone she'd known for many years from a previous job. When she told her boss of the decision, the woman said, "I wondered when this day would come. Go do what you do."

So the next phase of the journey began. Kimberly worked with the boss to create an exit strategy that was mutually beneficial, and then she threw herself headlong into creating a business. With her extensive background in team development and training, she knew she had the skills to make it work on her own terms. She began writing her book in October 2013 and started focusing on her own brand and image. She had already been a member of the chamber of commerce under the old company's brand but now was focused on strategically involving herself in leadership roles with visibility, and she began to connect with more people to build her business as a speaker, writer, and trainer.

Kimberly's book, *The Results Map*, is a straightforward planning guide that reflects the method she used herself in this process. She worked diligently to craft workshops and speaking opportunities where she could share the book and her thoughts on strategic planning with others, and things just started happening for her. Clearly, she also had solid relationships in many of the companies from which she came as well as industry credibility based on her own track record of success, which helped a great deal. But the bottom line is that she is now working doing something she loves while doing it on her own terms, and that has made all the difference.

Kimberly freely admits she made mistakes along the way. That period when she was so distant from her family still makes her cry when she talks about it, but she says, "I don't ever want to lose that feeling. It's a reminder." She believes it is important to "own your sh*t." Mistakes are part of the process, but "tough learning can come to something good." And, given the chance to go back, she does not think she would change much.

She also believes, as I do, that anyone can do anything they want to do if they want it badly enough and have a plan. Real strategy is not always tidy as we want it to be, and life sometimes gets in the way, but she said she struggles with people who play the victim card, preferring to approach challenges with a how-can-I-do-this attitude.

When it is time to move forward with a real strategy, it is important that you come to the table ready to plan and with a clear head. I believe that half of the battle, maybe more than half, comes with two words I love: prioritization and accountability. These are guiding terms in my life, and, if properly used, they can help me gain clarity about what I am doing and why. They can help you, too, to protect your goals and your strategy from being sabotaged by others.

First, I believe you have to decide what matters most to you. Why are you doing what you are doing, and what about it is important? You have to figure out what things in your life need to change and what things you will not change, or what you will change to accommodate the goals. Then you must put them in some kind of order. The tasks at the top of the list do not get compromised; the other things fit in around them.

Then you have to own your plan. Socialize it. Talk about it with the people in your life. Let people know what you are going to accomplish so that they do not derail your plans and because, in a best-case scenario, they can help you, motivate you, and maybe even keep you on task.

Prioritizing and being accountable are essential in planning and executing a strategy, and you will find it easier to make decisions in general if you know what matters most to you. That is certainly a takeaway from Kimberly Alexander's story, and it will serve you well if you try to move forward with that in mind.

Identifying goals is critical to executing a good strategy. Not having goals is like setting forth on a journey with no destination in mind. Certainly if you did that, you would arrive somewhere, but why would you ever do that? Goals are the guiding stars in the sky or on the horizon that help motivate us to move forward, however slowly. Goals are the reasons we do what we do; they are what we must prioritize if we are to achieve our dreams.

Goals can be small or "big, hairy, audacious goals," such as the ones Jim Collins advocates for in *Built to Last*. Whatever the case, if you don't have some, make them now. Think about what you want to achieve and what changes you want to see in your life. Then, and only then, can you truly walk in the direction of your dreams and see your life's wishes fulfilled.

Kimberly's goal? To help two hundred and fifty thousand people find the results they want! Amazing. She did not have a goal around money or material things; rather, her goal was to help others. In her own words, "If I am not making a difference, then I don't want to do it." She also said, "When you are authentic and real and make it about people first...yes, you need a plan because it happens!"

CHAPTER 6

Real Networking

> I happen to believe that America is dying of loneliness and
> that we, as a people, have bought into the false dream of
> convenience, and turned away from a deep engagement with
> our internal lives—those fountains of inconvenient feeling—
> and toward the frantic enticements of what our friends in the
> Greed Business call the Free Market. We're hurtling through
> time and space and information faster and faster, seeking
> that network connection. But at the same time we're falling
> away from our families and our neighbors and ourselves.
> —CHERYL STRAYED, *TINY BEAUTIFUL THINGS:*
> *ADVICE ON LOVE AND LIFE FROM DEAR SUGAR*

Networking has gotten a bad rap, I think. We have reduced our perceptions to two distinct kinds of networking. One is the old-school mixer. This is a miserable business or social gathering where individuals gather with the goal of meeting new people. They awkwardly stumble over introductions; make small talk about sports, weather, or business headlines; exchange cards; and then ditch the scene as fast as they can, counting "contacts" as successes.

Then, of course, there is social networking, which I talked about in chapter 1. It is a part of life now, and if you are in business in any form, I believe you have to have some plan about how you will approach it. Social networking is effective for building up your personal image or brand, and it is a way to sustain existing relationships—to some extent. However, there is no replacement for real human contact.

I have said it here before, as have some of the women I interviewed: "People do business with people they know, like, and trust." Period. People do business with people. I highly recommend a book by Tommy Spaulding: *It's Not Just Who You Know*. If we had featured men in this book, I definitely would have sought Tommy out for an interview. He has one of the most down-to-earth and real approaches to building relationships that I have ever seen articulated. He also has an amazing personal story. At its core, though, the book is about building real, lasting, and meaningful relationships with people. He ranks relationships and tells readers how he has approached building relationships that can change lives and communities.

This should be the goal, whether you buy into his approach or not. For as big as the world is—and it's pretty damn big—most things begin small, and most things grow from one individual's efforts to that of a few people. When people work together with common goals and interests, things get done; that is how the world is changed. That is how each of us can exponentially affect what is around us for ourselves and for others, through the power of others.

Getting to know people is not as hard as we make it out to be. In fact, I might argue, nowadays people are kind of starved for more human contact, for more friends, allies, and connections. In simple terms, the easiest way to start connecting is to find out what you have in common. Start with real conversation and *listen at least as much as you speak*. Practice the obvious things, such as remembering names and other details about people. I cannot tell you how many times people have commented on my memory of details about their lives. I think it is why I was a successful recruiter. I listen well and remember long.

Be yourself. Please, please, if you take only one thing away from this book, it is be real. Whatever that means, be you. No matter what your career is, you really don't need what Susie Wargin referred to (in media) as a persona. Just be a person. Make eye contact. Smile. Ask questions. Be positive.

Being positive is what brings me to the next story here, that of Angel Tuccy and the Experience Pros Network. Angel and her business partner, Eric Reamer, have built their entire business model on the power of positivity and networking. I have been in awe of their success for some time, and in the story that follows, you will see why.

The bottom line is that we will always thrive and find strength in numbers. We all need Kimberly Alexander's "crew"—a support circle around and behind us—to keep us moving in the right direction. None of us is an island, and it is much more fun and rewarding to be part of a community than to feel alone. Take time to build your own network. Though you may not realize it, you have one in the people you see, work with, buy from, live near, socialize with, go to church with, sit at kids' events with…you get my gist. There are people around you all the time. Whether you know them and leverage that is up to you, but you should try to connect and wait to see what great things can happen when you do!

Angel Tuccy

I think it is safe to say that I might not be writing this book if it were not for Angel Tuccy. Angel and her business partner, Eric Reamer, have a company called Experience Pros (www.ExperiencePros.com), and we met through our chamber of commerce in 2008. Angel and Eric are part of the same cohort, if you will. My company, DeCoste & Associates, and a few others all joined the chamber around the same time as we were launching our businesses. They stand out to me for a few reasons: mainly because they were among the first really friendly connections I made at the chamber, and now also because they have continued without interruption to build their company successfully and without sacrificing family and its needs.

Angel is an extraordinary woman. She is a force to be reckoned with when it comes to her determination; she is a petite powerhouse who has built an enormous brand with potential to do great things. She might be easy to overlook because she does not come across in an overwhelming way at all. (Neither does Eric.) She is a lovely, smiling, engaging, exceedingly positive person whom, I daresay, some may not take as seriously as they should. Beneath a bright, white smile and the glamor of her look is a woman who has worked tirelessly since 2008 to create the business she has. She has done so despite personal pressures, family matters, doubters, failure, and financial risk. She has done so with tenacity and grace, and talking with her about the journey reminds me why some of us choose to take the entrepreneurial path and why we must never give up.

On the day we met, I went to her corporate offices, which are in a twelve-story building overlooking the city. Sparkling white, snow-capped mountains in one direction and the beautiful Denver skyline in the other, it was a stunning panorama. She and Eric are on the radio daily and broadcast from the same building, so it makes sense that she is here. They now have nine employees. I am in awe of their success because I remember them way back when.

I first met them when we took a daylong executive retreat with the chamber and drove around town in one of those giant tour buses, looking at all kinds of new businesses. I ended up sitting next to Eric, who tried to explain their business. I must admit that I did not really understand. Come to find out, at that time, according to Angel now, the reason I did not understand is that they were still trying to figure out their own story.

Eric was a professional magician and the youth pastor at a church Angel attended, and Angel had been the event coordinator for a major annual golf tournament called the International. When that position went away, she went to work for Eric, ostensibly to help him book business. She told me that, at the time, she had no idea what to do to help him, and so she started cold calling. It did not take long to realize that was not the best approach.

She and Eric went back to the chamber for help and stumbled into a model that worked better. They realized, according to Angel, when it was time to renew their membership that they had not had great success at the chamber but that they were not alone. Nobody seemed to know how to *use* the chamber, she said. And that is where the idea started, and Angel went from employee to partner as she and Eric began building up the company.

Angel, ever seeking the right solution to her work-life struggle did not realize that she was on the brink of launching the new vision for the company as she sat at home one weekend trying to figure out their goals. As she told me, she got Eric to come over, and they pounded through a book on business fundamentals, realizing that they had completely missed the mark so far. What was the mission? Vision? Goals? If they did not know, how could they accomplish anything? And how many other businesses could benefit from this type of training? With that, they launched Experience Pros University and started training others.

It did not take long for them to realize they needed to scale their platform. Someone offered them a chance to broadcast on an Internet radio show, and shortly thereafter, a local radio program picked them up for a thirty-minute daily slot. That was six years ago. Now they broadcast daily for two hours. They have made some mistakes and missteps along the way, but they are on track.

What is the show about? It is about the Experience Pros Network and Directory. They have built a business model on small businesses and their customers that relies on the positive power of a solid network. Angel and Eric (the

Experience Pros) are on a mission to get people to spread positive feedback about businesses and create a community of businesses and consumers who rely on each other's endorsements—that is the Experience Pros Network and Directory.

It sounds a bit altruistic, I know, but the model is working. The Experience Pros invented "Fan Braggin' Friday," which is part of the radio show during which they invite listeners to call in and share stories of outstanding customer service they have experienced throughout the week and offer their endorsements. People call in! They use the hashtag #FanBrag and have created a local social media movement.

Angel will tell you that she and Eric are the most positive business on the radio. They choose to underscore good things in these cynical days. They focus on decent, honest people doing good, honest work, and they put the spotlight on them. It is an impressive model that is original and is truly helping them build their own successful business.

This brings me to the topic of networking and Experience Pros. Angel and Eric are masters of this skill. It seems to me that many people really loathe the whole concept, but I believe that is because they have a totally bogus notion of what networking is. I have come to this conclusion as I have watched Angel, Eric, and many others in my local community build strong and effective networks and circles of influence that drive and support their businesses.

Here is what networking is not and should never be. Networking is not heading into a roomful of people armed with a stack of business cards and an elevator speech or—worse—a pitch and trying to see how many people you can "hit" or how many cards you can get. Networking is not slimy. Networking should not be purely transactional at the onset.

Networking is a process of building business relationships and expanding your contacts by sharing of yourself and getting to know others.

Networking is easy and fun if you act human and behave naturally! Angel and I laughed about this quite a bit. "Since when," she quipped, "did it become normal to walk up to someone—especially a woman—with your eyes fully directed to her chest so you could read a name tag?"

We have both experienced that. You are standing there, eyes forward, and you see someone approaching you, but they are not looking at your face at all! Just the nametag. And heaven help them if they cannot pronounce your name. Then they finally look up and say, for example, "Is that pronounced *DeCoste* with an *e* or *a* sound at the end?"

In Angel's words, "That is not real life. That is not normal social behavior in the real world!"

What happened to making eye contact, smiling, extending your hand and saying, "Hi, I am Kim DeCoste; nice to meet you!" When they reply, by the way, you will get the pronunciation.

Our point in this conversation was that networking should be about finding out what we have in common, according to Angel. Find out where the mutual interests lie, where the dots connect. At the end of the day, one of my golden rules (which is not original, by any stretch) is the following: People do business with *people* they know, like, and trust.

I really mean it. Think about the choices you make even as a consumer. Do you go to the grocery store you go to just because it is convenient? My guess is that you go there, at least to some extent, because of the people. Whether it's the nice lady at the deli counter, the pharmacist, or the checkers with whom you chat regularly, you probably are more connected to the people than you realize. And, having done your homework on ratings and feedback, when you have a choice for a photographer or an insurance salesperson or a real estate agent, if you talk to a few before deciding, don't you go with the person you like the most? The person. Not the logo. Not the Facebook page. The person.

So it stands to reason that as a person and as a businessperson, the more people you get to know, like, and trust, the better off you will be. There are lots of cases in which this is true—whether they choose to do business with you, offer you a referral, or help you plan a professional transition of your own. Networking gives you a professional safety net, and if it is done correctly, networking can be one of the most valuable assets you have.

Along the way, one thing that Angel did was write a book. It was a small book that had a huge impact on me. I had always dreamed of writing a book, but when Angel did this back in 2009, the wave of self-publishing was just beginning, and I did not know anyone who had the gumption to actually do it. But what is remarkable is how she was able to leverage the book and build her brand. Her book is called *Lists That Saved My Life*, and while it did not win a Pulitzer, I found it to be informative on several levels. First of all, Angel really is a super list maker, and I was impressed by the level of organization she had. But beyond the lists themselves, she shared a lot about the behind-the-scenes life she and her husband, Jay, were living.

You see, Angel's transition from working at the golf tournament to being a successful entrepreneur was by no means an overnight success, *and* she was doing the dance of being a wife, mom, and aspiring business owner in a really authentic way. I neglected to mention that in 2008 when she and I met, she had twin sixteen-year-old daughters, a fourteen-year-old son, and her husband, Jay, was also starting a business. Talk about risk! They had whittled life down to sharing a car and were also fully committed to *not taking on debt*, which is amazing. In her book, she talks about how her lists and organization allowed her to save money and plan. I don't want to spoil the book entirely and retell it to you here, but things like paying for her daughters' braces all in cash still stand out to me. She and her family learned to prioritize and plan to such a degree that they were able to make this austere plan work.

Furthermore, there are tremendous lessons in time management, chore delegation, meal planning, and other aspects of daily life that Angel actually experienced as she was building her business. We talked about some of this in our interview for this book. She said that after working seasonally for the International for ten years, the transition to full-time entrepreneur was difficult. But she was devoted to her family so much that she was home every day those first few years between 3:00 and 5:00 p.m. to make sure the children were back and that homework and chores were started, and then she would head back out, as needed, to chamber networking events or to the office to finish off her day.

Now, though the kids are young adults and certainly don't *need* her as much as they once did, she still turns off her phone on weekends and makes sure she is fully devoted both to family and to downtime, which she covets even more than she used to. Angel believes that being *present* and being home are not the same thing and that she must work to ensure that she is taking time for both.

We talked a lot about mistakes. I think this is one area in which women struggle. We tend to beat ourselves up and carry guilt like extra baggage everywhere we go. It is not necessary. Angel recalled that the second year the business was trying to get up and running, she decided to take the summer off. I actually remember this because I was so jealous! But I was also amazed that she felt as if she could take the summer off while I was still scraping to build my business. Looking back, she realizes now that probably was not the best idea. It brought the business to a halt and set them back quite a bit.

At the time, however, she was feeling worry and guilt. It was going to be the last summer before her girls graduated from high school—potentially the last summer when everyone would be together as a family—and she had been working so hard building Experience Pros that she felt she owed them some time off. She told me, though, that she thinks if you asked her children now what they remember about the summer she took off, they likely wouldn't even remember it. In fact, she realized, her presence every night from three o'clock to five o'clock and her hands-on management of the household did resonate with them. She laughed about the fact that when it came down to it, the issue that forced her to take the summer off "was my baggage" and not theirs.

I can relate to this, and I am sure others can too. We sometimes measure our success and failure—especially with our children, I think—by ridiculous standards. Our children do not expect perfection. They are not born knowing what Martha Stewart or Rachael Ray—or whomever you compare yourself to when you are sizing up your domestic success—is like. Nor are they secretly reading *Lean In* or *Fast Company* or *Kiplinger* to assess your business acumen and financial prowess. Your spouse probably isn't either. *The people who love you and who are waiting at home at the end of the day or the week are just happy to have you home.* So be there when you can be. Cherish the time, even if it's in smaller chunks than you would like.

The work-life fantasy will never come into perfect balance. Never. Sometimes one side takes precedence, and sometimes it's the other side. Our challenge is just to make sure we keep the fluctuations in check and try not to lean too long or too hard one way or the other.

I asked her what motivates her, and she said it was probably faith. She believes there is a master plan, but she does not pretend to know what it is. She trusts that the journey, though not always easy, is carrying her in the right direction and that with hard work, dedication, and the right lists, she will find her way to the intended success.

"My reality," she said, "is this. This moment. This day. Right here. Right now. That's enough for me."

She acknowledges the missteps and the bumps in the road with humility and candor. But also notes that every once in a while, "like a God wink," some little something goes well or better than expected, and like a fresh wind in her sails, it helps her move forward and on to the next thing.

Roadblocks are real, however, and she and Eric have had a few. I asked her about that, about a time when there was not a lot of light in the tunnel, and how they survived. Back in 2010–11, the radio show was growing and the opportunity arose to syndicate outside of the Denver market. By coincidence, Experience Pros had partnered with another company, and they were coproducing part of each daily radio show. The other company's investment in Experience Pros was significant. Looking back, Angel said they really could not afford to turn it down. However, as quickly as it came up, quite unexpectedly at a point down the road, it disappeared and the partner went away. This left Experience Pros in a rough spot, with financial commitments beyond its means, and suddenly things were not looking too positive.

Watching Angel tell the story was impactful; I could see in her face, which is naturally lit by a smile most of the time, the stress and sadness of the memory. She said she and Eric were committed to continuing, and they negotiated payments so they could work through it. But the debt was a big albatross, and it took about a year. That year, she recalls, was brutal, and the odds felt as if they were totally stacked against them. The stress on their business relationship was smothering them, and, as she said, when you are in a partnership, "All you can hope for is that both of you never quit on the same day." However, at that point in time, they hit a wall, and both of them gave up.

She said it happened on a Friday. Both of them just lost their will to fight, and it seemed they were done. Financially, emotionally, and in every way, they had just exhausted themselves and each other. But as luck or the universe would have it, they had a commitment that weekend to appear somewhere together, so they could not just retreat to their corners and lick their wounds. They had to at least talk about it and put on their game faces for the public. Angel recalled the fear of failure and the sadness of thinking it was all falling apart. But, by some miracle or through the underlying strength of their convictions, they managed to survive. As they waded through the rubble of the situation, they realized there were some gems. There were some ideas still worth realizing and some resources not fully tapped. Most importantly, they realized they still wanted to try, once again. And they did.

Looking back, she sees the lessons they learned and realizes they are better for the experience, but that does not mean that period was easy to weather. They always say hindsight is 20/20, and I suppose that is true. Hopefully, though, as we learn more about how others have made mistakes, we can learn the easier way. In this case, one of the lessons I get from Angel's story (and from the Experience Pros success story) is that of tenacity.

For nearly eight years, Experience Pros has been inventing itself and iterating on its success. Meanwhile, Angel is still fully engaged with her family and well regarded in the business community. She has a story of perseverance and ultimately the confidence to stick to her guns and work through the challenges. By virtue of the fact that she has a business partner, too, she shows us that we do not have to go it alone in work or in life, and sometimes teaming up is the best way to do it.

I think there are many other lessons we could take away from the Experience Pros story. Until Angel and Eric write their own book to share more, you can tune in to their show on the radio in Denver or online. And, while you are writing your to-do list, you might pick up a copy of *Lists That Saved My Life*, especially if you have children. The chores list alone makes it worth the investment.

CHAPTER 7

Roadblocks Are Real

Life keeps throwing me curve balls and I don't even
own a bat. At least my dodging skills are improving.
—JAYLEIGH CAPE

When I conceived of this format for the book, I wanted to take stories of real women and fold them into material I had written about the topics in each of my chapters. What ended up happening, however, is that the stories, quite honestly, were way better and more interesting than the dry material I had written. So I have reverse engineered the idea, leaving the chapter headings in place as the themes and slotting the stories where I thought they fit best.

This chapter could be the whole book. It now features Avie Rosacci's story because it so clearly fits here, yet every woman I interviewed touched on this notion about getting past roadblocks and emphasized the challenges she's faced and how she overcame them. Resilience is a word I have used before, but it may not be a strong enough term. Tenacity is another good one. Patience, too, is an essential part of the mix.

There is no way to say it without sounding a bit trite, but the truth is bad things happen. What constitutes "bad" is also a point worth noting. I should have featured at least one story about someone who's overcome life-threatening illness or the illness of a child or spouse. Just today I found out about a friend battling ovarian cancer. She'll have a hell of a story to tell when she comes through it. Others have and do. I think those stories are meant for another book, though, as inspirational as they are. It would not feel correct for me to equate those challenges with the setbacks and roadblocks to which I refer here.

Back to the notion of everyday women, everyday life, and everyday problems, for our purposes here, when I refer to bad things that happen, I am talking about the things that take the wind out of our sails, not necessarily the things that bring us to our knees. And, so as not to diminish the impact of these setbacks, it's worth noting that when you are on an uncertain path—let's say to a change—and something goes awry or wrong, it's easy to lose courage, step back, or give up. You cannot let that be your story. You just can't.

There are not enough inspirational quotes or words for me to begin to rein them all in and somehow magically convey their power to you. I wish there were. At the end of the day, the measure of your success may be how many times you stood back up and kept trying to reach the goal, even if you did not reach it in the way you envisioned. Back to that notion of elasticity, sometimes goals change. But change is not a destination; it is a process, and you can't be changing if you are not trying. It's an action verb, not an adjective. (Okay, one could argue that change for women is a noun, too, but that's not the point.)

I said once at a conference that, as women, we should *own* change. We should proudly empower ourselves with that word. We are especially adept at handling it, and we should use that same strength when life puts up real roadblocks. The way we prepare for and overcome challenges in our lives is one of the most important skills we have. Whether it is through faith, friends, family, or some mix of those and other helps, we have to find a way to look past the roadblock to what lies ahead and keep moving forward.

Avie Rosacci

Avie Rosacci is a unique woman with a perspective that I thought would be interesting because she has literally grown up in her business. Avie is the only daughter in a family business that was started by her father and is now run by she and her two brothers. Tony's Market (www.TonysMarket.com) is a staple for excellent cuisine here in Denver. Tony Rosacci, Avie's father, is a legend who started with one little shop that was a converted 7-Eleven in 1978 and now has four locations as well as a catering company, which Avie started in 2004.

Avie's journey has been an interesting one, to say the least. You might think that because she grew up in a successful family business, she had an easy time of it, but the truth is that it has not been a cakewalk. The one thing Avie does concede, however, is that there are benefits associated with working with family. They take care of each other. At times when things have been tough, different resources have been available, and there is more flexibility than in some other cases. The family worked hard together through the recession, when a gourmet market was a luxury not everyone prioritized, and they worked with the extended families of their employees to keep things moving with minimal disruption and pain. They are a tight group, and that is special.

Avie herself is an inspiration. She has been through the wringer a few times and comes across now with such a positive, can-do attitude! In 2009, Avie had a rude awakening. She had remarried, and the two families had merged with a total of five kids. After fifteen years, her children were grown. Her business was five years old and was coming along, even through the recession. Then one day she came home from work to an empty house! I don't mean empty of people, though her husband had left. I mean empty empty! Almost everything she owned was gone. After sticking it out on the six-acre ranch for a year and a half, she sold the house and property, and when everything was settled, she literally had $300 left to her name. I cannot imagine how she came through it, but she did.

She tells the story in such a matter-of-fact way that it is hard to believe it is true. She really was blindsided by the loss of her possessions and the collapse of the marriage, but she had to move on, and she did. Just like that. She sold the home and readjusted her life and lifestyle and put her head down and worked. Her grown children were supportive as much as possible, but she really was on her own. She relied heavily on her family, but she did not get handouts or an easy ride.

Amazingly, she managed to carry on and rebuild her life. With the support of family and friends, she just went back to the drawing board, so to speak, and started over. She worked hard and learned a lot about letting go and figuring out what mattered.

On top of that, she has never turned away from a challenge. At one time she pursued barrel racing as a hobby. She said she spent far more than she ever won doing it but was happy to race against herself for best times. And because she had a fear of the ocean, what did she also decide to do to continue with her own self-improvement? Learn to scuba dive. I know it sounds crazy, but while she was rebuilding her life, she was building herself. This is the kind of thing I refer to when I say how lucky I feel to be surrounded by amazing women who inspire me. Really! Who does that? It's another case of, "If she can do it, so can I," and it makes me believe we can do anything when we set our minds to it.

Avie is in her fifties now. Her children are grown, and she married a wonderful man, Robert, four years ago. They are doing well, and she glows from the inside out when she talks about him and about their life together. She is also on the path to a new version of herself. She has recently returned to pursue a degree in nutrition. The oldest in the class, she is not at all intimidated; in fact, she is proud of her return to school and the fact that she believes she will be better for having gone back because many people in her family are not college educated at all. She stands out for that reason also.

Like so many women, Avie is in a constant battle with her weight. She has learned over the years that nutrition is an important part of how to maintain a balance that works for her, and, in fact, that is what brought her to the field of study. In 2010, she began having extreme anxiety attacks. She went to all kinds of doctors and tried both traditional and nontraditional medicine to remedy whatever was ailing her at the time. It turned out to be adrenal fatigue, and it was serious.

At that point, Avie was so focused on the business that she was not taking great care of herself. She had no work-life balance at all. It was all work. She was on call 24/7. Her largest client was the Denver Broncos—important to say the least! Catering may not sound like a stressful business compared to some, but people use caterers for special occasions and high-visibility events. With it comes demanding clients with top-shelf standards. Avie was at her clients' disposal, committed to the highest level of service. She had watched her dad build up the markets by always keeping the customer as the priority. He was her role model in that regard.

The pressure of it all was weighing heavily on her, and Avie was struggling to keep it all in check. Thankfully, she had a good friend who gave her the best advice she's ever gotten. One day, they had managed to escape to play golf. Avie's phone kept ringing, and she was so stressed and distracted that she was not even enjoying the beautiful day or the time with her friend Patty. That is, until Patty just looked at her and said, "You know, Avie, you're not *that* f***ing important!"

The comment hung in the air for a minute until they both laughed, but Avie realized Patty was right. She wasn't that important. None of this was worth what it was doing to her, and worst of all, it was her fault that it was having that effect.

This is a lesson I can absolutely relate to, and I bet many of you can as well. It is so easy to let our work encroach on every aspect of our lives these days that we make ourselves crazy. It is not only okay to turn off the cell phone once in a while, it is necessary. Whether you have family at home or not, there must be boundaries and limits. You can still keep an eye out for things that really are time sensitive, but we all have become way too connected to those devices. Few of us are that f***ing important!

As an aside, I went to a women's conference about five years ago where a panel was talking about work-life balance. I remember it clearly because high-profile women from the local business community were there. One, a senior-level telecommunications manager, was responsible for a global workforce and traveled extensively. Her name is Mary Ann. I remember her, in particular, because she also talked about the example we set for our children and our employees as women leaders when we are so compulsive and let work take over our lives.

She said, for example, that although she often checks e-mail and replies at odd hours of the day and night because of her international travel, she changes the send time on the e-mails so they are sent only during business hours. How many of us have worked for people who appear to be online and available 24/7? How many of us feel compelled to answer and be at their disposal as a result? It is not a good thing. Very few jobs are that important. Really, very few.

Back to Avie, the greatest lesson she said she has learned is *the importance of letting go.* She said she talked it over with her brothers, and they all agreed. It was okay to have a voice mail that referred to business hours and whom to call in emergencies outside of those hours. It was okay to delegate some of what she was doing to someone else. In fact, doing so allowed her to grow the business in a focused manner because she wasn't dealing with all the minutiae.

Looking back over the past few years, I asked her what advice she wishes she could have given or would give now, and she said, "Let go sooner."

She added, "Eventually, we will have to scale back even as business owners and replace ourselves. Why didn't I think about that sooner and make it easier on myself?" She went on to say, "The best leaders don't just lead; they develop people," helping them to overcome challenges.

She has learned that working from home once in a while is acceptable and that if you hire the right people, teach them well, trust them, and remain supportive of their efforts, you can build strong, dependable teams.

Avie really is another example—as I think about the *Sesame Street* song—of the "people in your neighborhood" who stand out because she is just one of the girls. She is down-to-earth, honest, and utterly real. I like her because she is a survivor in life, in love, and in business.

When we reconnected a couple of years ago, after having met and then not seeing each other for a time, I was stunned at how happy she looked. She was radiant! Turns out, she had her health under control and had married a fantastic man who is fully supportive of her in every way. Her business was growing, and she was moving into a new, beautiful house. It is amazing to me how quickly she was able to salvage it all and how low-key she is about the journey. Roadblocks are real. Challenges are real. Choices matter. And success—however you define that for yourself—is possible even under the most difficult circumstances, if you believe in yourself and keep trying.

CHAPTER 8

Real Success

> When you are young and impecunious, society conditions you
> to exchange time for money, and this is quite as it should be.
> Very few people are hurt by having to work for a living. But as
> you become more affluent, it is somehow very, very difficult
> to reverse that process and begin trading money for time.
> —WILLIAM REHNQUIST, US CHIEF JUSTICE
> COMMENCEMENT ADDRESS, BOSTON UNIVERSITY, JUNE 1988

This might be my favorite topic in this book. The stories here inspire me. Debra Fine, Michele Gross, and Jillian Gibbs are such interesting and different women. (I cannot wait for them to all meet each other!) In this chapter, like the previous one, I could have inserted a part of every person's story because each defines success differently and adds unique meaning. I believe Debra, Jillian, and Michele fit here best, though, in part because they have created such different business models.

I realized after the book took shape that this one has a heavy emphasis on entrepreneurs, and that was accidental. It just happens that the women I know in the circles in which I operate who seemed to jump out at me for this first book have that in common. That is not to suggest, by any means, that the only way to be successful is to start your own business.

For these women, however, it was the right choice in the face of challenge. For these women, it allowed for the elasticity that helped them give more to their families in some ways, though there was an ebb and flow as the converse was also sometimes true. The flexibility of the goals associated with what they were doing was important.

Back to the touchstone of priorities, the common thread among these three women and, indeed, with all the women I spoke to is that success was being able to attend to whatever seemed to be most pressing at the time. For some it was children first, work second. For others, work took priority and family the backseat. The point is, as long as what the women were doing was in alignment with what they really wanted, they felt successful. *In other words, success occurs when achievement meets expectations.* I know that sounds too obvious, but it is true, and it is not as easy or intuitive as you might think.

When what you are doing falls into place with the goals you have set—no matter what those goals are—you will feel success. I believe that is also why it is important to have at least some of the goals be about quality of life and other subjective things that you can gauge for yourself. We will address this more in the next chapter with Angela Cody-Rouget, but if the balance of your bank account is the only measure of success you have, you may never feel as if you are making it. You cannot always directly control that.

The women in this chapter exemplify these points. Each took on the challenges of the business she was creating and put herself out there to accomplish what she could without a specific number in mind but rather with an idea of what success would look like. Working independently and directly with clients while expanding the business was a goal for one. Raising kids and being able to have financial security and time with them during the day was another's goal. One just wanted to see how far she could take the dream without taking on too much risk or disrupting her family life. Each of these women realized her goals, and all are successful, though differently so.

Ultimately, it may come back to the notion of minimizing regrets. There are bunches of sayings about what people will regret. Not the missed meetings, that's for sure. Some say it's the things we did not try. I think success must be first and foremost a state of mind. It is the internal peace that we find when we are doing something that makes us feel good about our work—no matter what that is—and allows us to enhance and enjoy our lives outside of work as much as possible. Some people even achieve a level of success that is really marvelous when work and life are part of the same rhythm, with no clear distinction or stopping point between them. They "harmonize" (as Susie Wargin suggested) or mix (as you will hear from Angela), and they become just...life. The sooner we can find a way to define success for ourselves in a realistic and attainable way, the sooner we will feel truly successful.

Debra Fine

Debra Fine is a best-selling author and renowned international speaker who is a member of my Rotary Club. I have known her for about four years, and she is one of my greatest inspirations—and now, I think I can say, a mentor and a friend. Her story is one of challenge, survival, and success.

Debra's professional orientation was toward engineering nearly forty years ago when she was starting her career. Eventually it morphed into recruitment, which is not surprising because she is a remarkably strong communicator and had the ability to understand the challenging field of engineering. She, like many women, married and started a family, and eventually her energy and effort went from work to the children and her husband. She was in the background as his business launched and grew while bringing up her two babies. Then, as so often happens, a real roadblock slammed into her. Divorce. A tricky, complicated divorce.

She found herself alone with two small children, no financial resources, and an unclear future. I recently heard her tell the story again, and she said her greatest concern was making enough money to somehow not only support the children but also keep them from having to be put in day care. Now that may seem silly to those of us who used day care, but from her perspective, the children had already been through enough; they had never been in day care, and she thought that would be too tough on them. Fair enough. We all have to make these kinds of decisions for our children and by our own standards. She set out to find a way to work evenings when she could hire high school girls to sit with the children because that, she said, was normal for them. Mom and Dad used to go out, and they were comfortable with babysitters like that.

Debra began by responding to an ad by Colorado Free University, which was seeking instructors. She knew she had marketable skills; she just needed to dust them off. And so she began by creating a course geared toward engineers on the art of communication. The class was a success. Notoriously introverted techies appreciated her direct manner, knowledge of their field, and charming and intelligent demeanor.

Fast-forward a bit, and Debra decided to capture her ideas in a book, *The Fine Art of Small Talk*, which became a huge hit! Suddenly, she was in the driver's seat of her career and her life again. She was able to scale her work to accommodate the children, and she was on a path to a nice living. Debra self-published her first book, but it was picked up by a publishing company after a bidding war between two publishers. The book is a simple, concise, excellent piece of work that has been translated into multiple languages all over Europe and Asia.

It has not been an easy path, but she seems to have few regrets. She also met the love of her life along the way. Her husband, Steve, is a periodontist, and he also struggled through a divorce. When they met and eventually married, just over twenty years ago, they were effectively starting from scratch with a blended family and lots of goals still to accomplish. But they never looked back. And, divorce aside, Debra does not have regrets about much at all. She freely admits that she chose to be a housewife. She could have remained an engineer or a recruiter, but she chose her family because that felt like the right thing for her at the time.

When I asked her about the work-life balance, she said there is no "life balance; just life." She believes we must do the best we can with what we have and find our own version of what that balance looks like.

Further, Debra wanted to talk about defining success your own way. She is often asked why she doesn't do more, grow her brand, expand her professional reach, and so on. Her simple answer is, "Because I don't want to." She is approaching another big birthday this year and is a role model of grace and confidence. That is not to say life is perfect or work isn't hard for her sometimes. Of course it is. She talked about the rigors of traveling across time zones and then having to force herself to bed early so she can be primed and ready to go on stage sometimes as early as seven o'clock or seven thirty in the morning.

The beauty of it is, however, that she is defining her success her way. Now she is not working purely out of necessity but rather from the heart. Her definition of success involves having all the bills paid and some financial freedom. She has put her two children through college, and one daughter is ready to get married. The money for the wedding was set aside long ago.

Now, as a 1K traveler on United Airlines, Debra enjoys assignments all over the world, and she brings Steve along whenever she can. Last year she had nine jobs in

Singapore. She sometimes has the benefits of free accommodations through her work, so she has more time and money for the things she cares about. She is an avid cyclist, so she and Steve tool around the world by bike, and, as a Rotarian, she is able to do great work through Rotary as she travels as well.

Debra's life is not everyone's dream life. It is hers. Her greatest achievements? Clearly her children. Recently her daughter told her that she wants to have her life. Her kids have watched her struggle and build her success slowly and through hard work. They have watched her be there for them as she was teaching and helping others. They have watched her build a second marriage over twenty-one years that is solid and happy in a lovely home, and she remains active in the community.

Debra reminds us that anything is possible if we are willing to do the hard work and stick to it. And she reminds us not to settle for too much BS along the way! For that, I can only say thanks to Debra for leading the way! (To find out more about Debra and her work, please visit www.DebraFine.com.)

Michele Gross

I have talked many times about the importance of a plan. Strategy is essential in business and in life. You have heard my story about how I decided to leave a corporate job and start my services company. Michele Gross's story is quite different; she has done something more complicated in that she turned her hobbies into a design and distribution business.

Many people talk about Peter Drucker's principles as they relate to SMART goals. That is the acronym for "specific, measurable, assignable, realistic, and time lined." Those criteria are certainly important. Take a good look at what you want to achieve. Can you articulate it clearly? Can you find ways to mark incremental success? (This is especially important for big goals. It is hard to stay motivated over long periods of time and with enormous goals if you cannot see and celebrate progress.)

If it is an organizational goal, can you assign it to a specific person and make that individual accountable? Or can you assign subtasks of the goal to several people? Finally, what is the due date? Goals should have deadlines. All of these criteria are important.

However, in the real world, nothing is as tidy as an acronym. In the real world, ideas evolve and take shape sometimes in the not-so-black-and-white world for which Drucker is aiming. Sometimes the goals are less lofty and more about "seeing what comes next" or what is around the corner and then just having the guts and the tenacity to take one more step toward a vision.

Such is the case for my friend Michele Gross. Michele and I met on the board of our kids' PTO in 2008. She struck me immediately because she is pretty, smart, stylish, and funny in addition to being extremely approachable. I had struggled to make friends with some of the mommy crowd at the school because we did not have a lot in common. I have never been a stay-at-home mom, and in 2008, I was trying to get my business off the ground. So while I was present for school functions and meetings, I was always watching the clock and often had my mind in other places. Michele stood out in the mommy crowd and was the PTO treasurer. She was organized and analytical, and she knew how to use Excel!

When she and I met, she was a stay-at-home mom with two boys, and I knew she was into scrapbooking and card making. (She is one of those people who sends out handmade holiday cards, for goodness sake!) At that time, she was not yet in her business.

Michele's story, however, is one of my favorites because it is an example of a hobby-turned-business by an everyday person whose strategy was just to see what would happen if she continued down the path. Michele did not have a business plan. She did not map out a strategy or benchmark goals. Her real-world story could be anyone's story. She just started asking questions and following her gut. Now she has a nearly three-year-old business that is thriving, and she is the master of her own universe.

Michele started scrapbooking, like so many people do, when her first son was born, nearly sixteen years ago. She loved doing it but said she enjoyed card making more because she got to share her work rather than just putting it into a book (that rarely got looked at). In the meantime, she and her family relocated from Las Vegas to Colorado, and she was settling in and making new friends.

One of those friends also had a blog. Blogs were new, but Michele was fascinated by the idea of having people follow her crafting activities, so she asked herself the eternal question, "If she can do it, why can't I?" Shortly thereafter, she was on a business trip with her husband, and after walking around awhile, she returned to her hotel room and Googled "blogging." She explored options, chose a free platform (Blogger), and published her first blog. She had immediate success.

The community of people with the disposable income and time to pursue scrapbooking, stamping, and card making is a specific one, and Michele knew immediately how to connect with them. Her blog, CAS-ual Friday Stamps, was off and running, and soon she had hundreds of followers. The little brand was making progress and building an audience all by itself, and she kept taking the baby steps needed to move it forward toward being a business.

Michele freely admits that there never really was a plan; rather, her strategy was to find out what she needed to do and then, at each inflection point, see how she could move forward without spending too much money and without too much difficulty. Michele did have some background in retail as a buyer, and she also had worked, prior to having children, for a short time as a field representative for Gucci. Thus, she was not without *any* experience, but she really had no idea what it took to start a business. In her brand name, CAS-ual Friday, the "CAS" stands for "clean and simple," and that is how she approached building her business. One small step at a time. Clean and simple.

She also found out that her new niche industry was not the most supportive one. The people who had success did not want the competition, so they remain tight-lipped about how they got into it and succeeded. As a result, Michele did not have any real mentors or guidance. Her husband worked in a high-level position in the retail industry, so he was able to help to some degree with some of the financial and business planning, but she really grew the business on her own and without outside help.

It was fascinating to hear her explain how she had to define the challenges in front of her, breaking them down into increments she could understand. It is not as if she could do a Google "how-to" search and get all the information handed to her! She wanted a stamping business but did not have the first clue about how to approach it.

She began making inquiries regarding the manufacturing of the stamps and dies (as in the tools used for cutting and shaping paper) and was participating to a greater degree on the design side. Gradually, Michele saw she was gaining traction. She was submitting her card designs into challenges sponsored by people in the industry who were looking for fresh ideas. She won a few challenges and even threw a challenge of her own to drive visibility.

Still, though, as she said, at the beginning there were no earnings; it was all "just ink and paper." She was blogging, designing, and building a fan base, but it did not really become a business until she launched a website for sales. The deciding moment came on a plane home from an industry trade show in 2010 for the Craft and Hobby Association. She got to see others who were making money at her hobby, and all the way home she wondered, "Can I make it work?" On that flight she had the "if-she-can-do-it-why-can't-I?" moment. She took the leap of faith.

One thing she did know was that she wanted her products to be made in the United States. She had done the research and knew a few things: most of the people in her target demographic were in the middle of the country. Most of those people were middle-aged and had disposable income. Stamping is not an inexpensive hobby, so these individuals were already paying a premium, and she believed that having the products made here would be a selling point. But, she wondered, who makes stamps and dies?

At the trade show, she'd met several nice people who were generally supportive, but when she reached out to them, they would not share any information about where their products were made. Finally she found a place to which she submitted her designs for manufacturing. It was a big moment in the life of her business, and she was excited and looking ahead to the launch of her product. But, of course, roadblocks are real, and she was about to hit one.

She got an e-mail from the company that it would be going dark for a short time to do a physical move of its facility. She waited and waited to hear back after the date indicated. After not hearing anything further, she eventually reached out and was told the company was working on her products. A couple of weeks later, same thing. No feedback or updates, and she called again. Same answer: "We are working on them." Finally, frustrated, she got someone on the phone who admitted that during the move the company had lost her designs!

Michele was devastated. This was one of the moments in which she almost gave up. She was so frustrated and had put so much time and energy into this business and felt the setback was too much to handle. Thankfully, she was able to find backups of the designs, and even though she was now six weeks behind her goals, she decided to press on.

Her logic? Well, she was the only one on a deadline. Nobody else had been disappointed yet. She had been teasing the launch of the new product line on her blog but had not announced it yet, so after she calmed down, she realized the setback was not visible to anyone else. She just needed to find a new manufacturer and start again. So that is what she did.

All in all, the process (research, taking online classes to learn how to use Illustrator to make the designs, finding a new manufacturer, and finally having the product in her hands) took nine long months. The same time, Michele said with a laugh, as having a baby!

In October 2012, she launched her products, and on the first day, she did $1,000 in sales! On the second day, she said, it was $100. And so it goes. Up and down and highly seasonal, she is now in a business that is successful but tough to predict. When she creates designs, some fly off the shelves and some do not. Now having the data from two whole years in business, she is better able to see trends and plan ahead, but she is still learning as she goes. Michele has a notebook with her wherever she goes.

She said, "Inspiration comes at the most inopportune times. I could be sitting watching one of the boys wrestle, and something will grab my attention and the idea is born. It could be a song or a pattern on a dress in the store. One thing I love about this is that it is such a creative business. And there is a part of me that likes that little nervous feeling after I send in a set of designs and wonder where the next inspiration will come from!"

Michele is in a unique position now of having built a business that she is able to control, and she has her hand on the nozzle as she tries to figure out what's next. She has approximately 1,500 Facebook fans and an equal number on her blog. Her business is steady and trending upward, which is good after the tough economic years we have had. Stamping is a discretionary expense for those who do it, and when money is tight, it is not a high priority for hobbyists.

Things are looking up, and Michele is looking ahead. She has added wholesale to her website, so she has expanded from just direct retail to the customers. She is still handling all of the design, processing, and order fulfillment on her own from her dining room and basement. She is a one-woman band and happy to stay that way for now. Her husband jokes that he will retire and she will support the family on her "little business" someday. She will have her two sons at home for a few more years, so she wants to be present for them as much as possible. She understands, however, that as they grow up and move out, their lives will change, and she does not know yet whether she wants to keep things as they are or expand.

Controlling the flow is her challenge at the moment. She has to wisely manage costs of inventory and orders. She cannot afford a big burst in business, either, as she has only so much bandwidth. Too much business is as scary to her as too little. When I asked what motivates her, she smiled and kind of shrugged as she said, "The fact that I don't have to do this but I get to do it is what motivates me the most." For now, she is sitting pretty in her niche market, keeping it real and keeping it going, with her feet on the ground and her eyes on the dream.

Not everyone can be like Michele. She has the right mix of motivation, knowledge, discipline, and support from her family to be able to turn a hobby into a business, but she is also really just the woman next door. Like all of the women in this book, she is someone just like you or me who has found a way to make her work and her life fit together by taking a risk, having a vision, doing her homework, adjusting to challenges, sticking it out, and pursuing a dream. She embodies the "if-she-can-do-it-why-can't-I?" spirit, and her story could be your story if you are willing to put yourself out there, get real, and go for it.

Jillian Gibbs

If you ran into Jillian Gibbs, she would absolutely catch your attention the moment she laughed. She has one of those laughs that lights up everything and everyone around her. She is down-to-earth and approachable and easy to talk to. You probably would not guess that she founded and built a $20-million company called Advertising Production Resources (APR). I met Jillian in 2010 while I was working for a small media production company, and we piloted a series for entrepreneurs. She came in for an interview, and I was struck by how normal she seemed for someone who had achieved such a level of professional success. She has not changed since then; she has just achieved more.

Like all of the women featured in this book, Jillian does not come from an affluent family. Her parents were hard workers and set a great example, and they instilled in her basic values that inform her perspective to this day. Her father was a custodian in a New York City public school for thirty years, and her mother worked her way up to executive director for the Girl Scouts in Manhattan and Brooklyn. Neither of her parents attended college or had their own business. They divorced when Jillian was eleven years old.

Every woman I have spoken to for this book has cited her mother as a person—if not *the* person—she most admires. Jillian is no exception there, either. She remembers her mom learning as she went along and standing in front of large groups of people and being able to "pay attention to the room, so she could respond to them in a way that resonated with them."

Jillian's father was also tremendously influential to her as she was growing up. He did not care what she ended up doing for a living; he just wanted her to be happy and be the best at whatever she did. For his part, he was "the highest-paid, best-known custodian at the time and was very much loved by the faculty of the schools...students, and families." Though Jillian has achieved success in business, you might find it interesting to know she went to college to study opera! Jillian does credit her stage and theater training with helping her to have the poise now required in her leadership role at APR.

After college, she returned to Manhattan, where she worked in advertising and auditioned for the theater. She sang and danced on cruise ships and in off-Broadway productions in New York, but her day job was in advertising, and she got a break when she landed at Unilever (the second-largest consumer products company in the world, following Procter & Gamble).

At the age of twenty-one, she was the assistant to the head of advertising production, who became her mentor. By the time she was twenty-five, her mentor, Al Tennyson, retired, and she convinced the management at Unilever that she should take over his role. They gave her one year to prove herself and hired an assistant for her. Jillian successfully expanded the role to include print, television, radio, and digital production. She married at age twenty-eight and left New York, and though the marriage ended after four years, she credits it for getting her to Colorado, where she founded APR—with Coors Brewing Company as her first client.

In the interview we did at the media company with Jillian for the show a few years ago, the host dubbed her "The Accidental Entrepreneur," which is fitting. Contrary to all of my convictions about the importance of a plan and taking careful, measured steps, Jillian did not set out to do what she has done. She did not have a business plan; she followed her instincts and just let her work speak for itself. She is practical and unpretentious, and she has just grabbed opportunities as they presented themselves.

The story evolves simply. When Jillian got to Colorado, she reached out to Coors to see if she could handle their advertising production needs, and they agreed. After three years, she was covering all their US and international television commercial productions and had to hire staff to help her. Then she was ready to take on more clients, and Coors supported that. Though she was never a Coors employee, for eleven years she was known as "the Coors girl," and then, in 2007, Coors fired APR. That was the catalyst that catapulted her company, and she has not stopped growing by double digits since. APR now has 110 employees in thirteen cities around the world. Jillian has built a company where people want to work and typically try to stay, and business is booming.

I know I have said several times throughout the book that success does not necessarily equal money, but I thought it important to include a story of someone who has achieved financial success at this level without defining herself or her success by dollars and cents. That's Jillian, for sure. She is actually low-key about the success she has had, though she does not dismiss the amount of effort she has poured into it over the past fifteen years. APR is three times bigger than its nearest competitor, and she recently changed the title on her business cards to say "Global CEO & Founder." That is no small statement.

What is the secret of her success? Well, she believes in the final analysis that "people like to work with people they like." I agree. She has built trust and loyalty with her clients, and now she is working on a new methodology that has clients interacting with one another, even when they might be competitors. She gets clients "networking with each other and relationship building in a closed group" and finds that great things come of it.

She's also worked hard to build APR into a firm with a family feel to it. "Communication is key," says Gibbs, and she has finely tuned her ability to get a sense of what is needed by paying attention to clues. Her role now, with the staff as large as it is, is to set the vision and focus more on "coaching and inspiring key people." She also works on the business development side and on the hiring, ensuring that they really do hire people "who truly are creative." The right mix of talent, motivation, and guidance also allows her to set the bar higher and charge more. People pay for the quality that APR produces.

Jillian firmly believes that "you are only as good as your people," so she works hard to ensure that they not only find but also keep the talent they identify. With an 86 percent retention rate, it would seem she's doing something right. She puts a high value on the corporate culture, spending a quarter of a million dollars on an annual meeting to bring everyone in the organization together and insisting on "monthly huddles" in which the teams across the globe get on conference calls to talk about the latest industry issues.

Admittedly, she finds herself faced with decisions "for which there is no playbook," such as the recent death of a longtime employee or the prolonged illness of another. In the end, she said, you have "got to be able to be good to your people and do what feels right." She realizes that as CEO, the "choices I make affect the way we live our lives." She takes that seriously and is thoughtful in her leadership. She stopped sending e-mails on the weekend because her people felt they needed to stop what they were doing and respond, which meant their weekend was disrupted and they might eventually face burnout. So by modifying her behavior, she has been able to lead by example, and her work-life balance is key to longevity and success.

Reflecting back on her father, too, she notes that one big lesson he taught her was, "People have no color, and all people at all levels [from the CEO to the dishwasher] should be treated with respect." Jillian is mindful of this at all times and has instilled it in the corporate culture as well.

Jillian is not a huge fan of milestones. She said that to her, they create pressure, so she avoids investors or boards to allow her the flexibility to go with the flow. Her business grew organically, though the growth did not just happen by luck or chance. Rather, thoughtful progress and consistently offering great service has been the key. When asked, "How big do you want to get?" she answered, "How many more people can we give it to?"

Fifteen years into it, Jillian is faced with a new challenge. She has come to see that the company is a success with a strong management team, and her focus is now to focus more on herself personally. Her identity has been tied to the business for such a long time that she has not really defined herself in any other way for fifteen years. The challenge is to work on her own brand and her personal life. She wants to travel and has set a goal to live abroad for a month and start dating again. It's hard, she said, to slow down. She is certainly still enjoying work, so she is not thinking about stepping away. However, she wants to focus on the other parts of her life.

Extracting herself from her business identity is challenging. She talked about a leadership conference she attended last year with peers of the same level of professional success. Absent the conversations about work, and without her company name and title on her nametag, she struggled to be "just Jillian." That experience is part of what helped her decide to shift her focus.

Like all of us, she finds that the work-life balance is elusive. It has been "all or nothing" for her over the past several years, and she is looking at ways to bring the focus back to herself, her personal goals, and her needs. It's interesting, too, that Jillian is eminently confident in her work and in her company, but when she is talking about herself, she is quite low-key and exceedingly modest. She is optimistic about the future; she has started dating again and is enjoying getting to know people outside of the work circle. For her, as with others I have spoken with, building a network of close friends is also important.

One thing she mentioned that I would not have thought of is that it is tough to develop personal relationships with people after achieving a certain level of success, just because few can relate to the universe in which she operates. Also, I am guessing, there is some intimidation factor for those she meets, both in building a love life and in expanding friendships. Her professional success does not define her from her perspective, but it may define her to others. She said that, even in dating, it is frustrating to go out with people who have done their research and leave no stone unturned with all the available resources online. It is awkward to try to get to know people who already think they know you. But she is working on it and is enjoying the process.

Jillian laughs at herself easily and draws you in when she speaks. Her nature is warm and sincere, but it is clear that she is a strong person. She is getting bolder about reaching out to her clients, the CEOs of major *Fortune* 100 companies, and talking to them directly about their businesses. It was not until recently that she felt she was ready to command that kind of attention. But she does and should. She is somewhat in awe of APR's success, recalling a time when a part-time CFO she hired was asking her if she was ready to be a $10-million company someday.

Her response, she said with a laugh, was, "Get the f*** outta here!" She certainly did not expect to surpass that figure, but here she is.

I was happy to ask my favorite question to her that I have asked all of the women I talked to for this book. What advice would you give your twenty-five-year-old self? Once again, she rang in with *nearly the exact answer every woman has given me*, each without talking to the others: (1) See the world. (2) Be brave and be bold. (3) Above all else, just try.

No person in this book is more important or impressive than any other. What I am struck by is the similarity in their outlooks. This must be one of the takeaways, at least for me. Real success is different for each of them. None of them has the same vision for herself as the other fourteen women featured here. *They all do have a common belief in themselves, however, that is not unwavering but is renewable.* Does that make sense? Each of them admits to some insecurity or uncertainty at some point, but they all seem to have a wellspring of faith in themselves, at least at this stage of their lives, from where they can draw strength, confidence, and courage.

None of the women featured feels she has achieved success easily. They all concede that success was time-consuming and that they often either lacked a plan or deviated from the plan such that they felt they were sailing in uncharted waters. This was a common sentiment. What strikes me, though, is how much all of these women talk about relying on instinct and trusting their gut feeling when it came to making decisions or taking risks. What I heard over and over was that they had to learn not only to hear that inner voice but also to believe in it and to believe in themselves. Some had spouses or partners who were "in the way"; some had spouses or partners who stood in support. In the end, however, every woman I talked to here has achieved her success on her own.

Success, therefore, might just be that—achievement of any goal to your own satisfaction so that you believe enough in yourself to raise the bar and try again. It is still different for each of us, but there is a common theme of having accomplished something in your own right and gaining confidence in the process. If you are struggling to find out what to change or how to change, start small. Challenge yourself incrementally. Every woman I talked to for this book agrees that none of us knows what her potential really is until we stretch and just go for it, which brings me back to an old favorite quote: "What would you attempt to do if you knew you could not fail?" Indeed, that is the question.

CHAPTER 9

Keeping It Real

I do not like the man who squanders life for fame;
give me the man who living makes a name.
—EMILY DICKINSON

One of the great challenges we face as we pursue our dreams and achieve success is staying grounded, I think. It is easy for success to go to our heads and change us. That is one area in which all of the women I have featured in this book are impressive, despite the varying levels of success they have achieved. They remain approachable and have not let their success transform them. They have also kept their priorities straight (once those were identified) and managed to keep their feet on the ground and their eyes on their dreams.

It is especially hard to know how to go through the necessary day-by-day things we have to do to keep the dream moving along, when those steps do not feel easy or as if they are part of the bigger plan. Finding the motivation for slowly evolving success is hard, and staying connected to the energy required day after day to make a vision become a reality is a great challenge. Sometimes the necessary steps are not easy or pleasant, but there are not many shortcuts.

The two women in this chapter resonated with me for this topic because of two things they share in common, which were so pervasive as they told their stories. One is tenacity, and the other is a spiritual or faithful side. I was not sure if discussion of God or religion would be part of this book, and I am not here to dictate on the topic one way or the other. Faith is deeply personal.

Angela Cody-Rouget's story is one of the best I know. Angela continues to succeed as she is expanding her company nationally. She is achieving tremendous recognition in the national media and through several veterans' and small business competitions, and she is marching ahead, having always done whatever was necessary to further her dream, but armed with deep faith and conviction that God must be first in her life.

Sue Kenfield has achieved success as a solo-preneur consulting with organizations to "drive down drama and dysfunction." She has taken a careful approach to building her career and credentials, and she is more than qualified in her field. She, too, is deeply guided by faith, though perhaps in a more spiritual sense than that of traditional religion. Sue discusses the value of introspection and stillness. She appreciates the value of listening to your own inner voice as you make choices, and she is vitally aware of the connection, at least for herself, to spiritual, physical, and professional wellness and success. Both ladies offer fresh perspectives on the ideas of "keeping it real" and help us expand our perceptions about what matters most, as we strive for our dreams.

Angela Cody-Rouget

The story of Angela Cody-Rouget and her journey to build a company called Major Mom (www.MajorMom.biz) is one of my favorites and could probably be built out as a book all by itself. Angela is another person, like Angel Tuccy, whom I met through the chamber of commerce and who launched her business around the same time I did. Like Angel, I have kind of benchmarked my success and growth against hers. She and Angel are such tremendous success stories in my mind that I couldn't *not* include her story here. I have also consulted for her company, so I have worked with her and had the good fortune to learn from her as well.

Angela is a one-of-a-kind business leader whose feet are firmly on the ground. She is deeply faithful and puts God in the center of all that she does. She is a devoted mother and wife, and she is on a mission to liberate us all from the burdens of too much stuff and poor organization. I have never met anyone like her, and I admire her a great deal for all that she does and the approach she has to life.

Angela's first career was with the US Air Force, where she served for twelve years as a satellite operator and missileer. She achieved the rank of major. She was dedicated to her work and her country, and she enjoyed her life. She met her husband, Frederic, and in 2003, with the birth of her first child, he gave Angela the nickname "Major Mom." She continued to work and had a second child in 2005, but by then, the strain of trying to maintain a demanding career and raise two children was starting to show. Angela and Frederic decided she should resign her commission and focus on the family for a few years. Frederic was in the real estate business, and things were fine, so they took the chance, and Angela became a stay-at-home mother. She did enjoy the time at home, but she was eager to do a little something on the side, both to fill some of the time and to contribute financially.

Organization is in Angela's blood. The family she grew up in moved sixteen times, and she moved eleven more times as an adult, so she has always believed in traveling light and not getting too attached to possessions. She began her organizing business in 2006 to help others liberate themselves from too much stuff, realizing how many women were drowning in things while continuing to add to the piles. She called the problem "affluenza" (a term born from a lawsuit unrelated to her or her business and subsequent books about the affliction of wealth), an illness of the affluent, who spend their lives amassing possessions and then stressing about how full—literally—their lives and homes are with things in need of organization.

The period between 2007 and 2010 was what Angela called a rough ride. As was the case for so many of us, the recession hit, and Frederic's real estate business was struggling. He said they needed to go "back to the drawing board" to figure out what they really were going to do, and Angela decided to build the little organizing business into something bigger, but that was not going to be easy.

At one point, she found herself working as a waitress on the side to help the family while they both did what they could to keep things afloat. Her husband took a job at their church's preschool so that they could get 50 percent off tuition, and he taught there while at Word of Life Academy for three years. Angela also worked at the preschool helping with the after-school program. They downsized their lives and went back to apartment living and the basics.

This is the perfect example of what I mean when I say all things are possible, but we do face challenges and choices, prioritization and accountability. Angela was determined, however, that her company, Major Mom, would grow. And it did.

When I asked her whom she admired, she said she looked at the success of Mary Kay Ash for motivation. Mary Kay had built her business out of necessity but also to help others. Angela liked the model and wanted to help other women who were trying to stay home with their children find a way to do some work on the side and keep their families as the number-one priority. Family is central to the Major Mom model, and it is Angela's goal to continue to bring peace and joy to people's lives through organizing. She now has sixteen employees and has expanded to four states with employees who have relocated and started in new markets. She also has a business partner, Mandy Pinkston, who complements Angela's skills by managing all the company leads and client-care issues while Angela focuses on new business development and expansion. It is finally working for them.

Angela is based in Phoenix now, so we did our interview for the book via Skype, and it was a great conversation. She went through the headings of all of the chapters and kicked off the conversation by saying, "What I think makes a businesswoman successful, Kim, is mastering all of these ten chapters." I agree!

We began with what she thought is one of the worst mistakes she sees all the time in business, and that is lying. Many women lie to everyone *including themselves* about how successful they are, about where they are in their journey, about income, or about the number of clients they have. It is hard, especially as a new small business, to talk about the status of the business honestly with everyone, but Angela believes the lying is doing more harm than good.

As she said, "It is hard to be authentic in any way if you are lying." She credits a man named Thomas Hopkins with giving her the remedy to this. When people ask how things are going, the answer should be, "Unbelievable!" That more accurately reflects the roller-coaster ride and does not say whether it's unbelievably good or bad. Just unbelievable. It is honest, at least.

The truth, she believes, is that the great burden still comes from the fact that the majority of the world still defines success purely on "the number of dollars in the bank." Angela believes—for herself—that success is taking the kids to school and being there to pick them up. She is happy to help with homework and cook dinner and sit down together to eat. Once the kids are in bed, she can get more work done, and that is success for her. She does bring in money to support her family, but money is not *the* defining factor; it is *a* defining factor. The choices we make define our ability to succeed, whatever that means for you, but you have to know what matters to you. Most likely it is not just money.

Regarding the issue of work-life balance, she believes "the term sets us up for failure" because, like others I have mentioned, she feels it is a "work-life mix" or "work-life harmony" that we should seek. Periods of days, even weeks, cannot be all about the kids. Work is real. Deadlines are real. When work does have to be the priority, it is a chance to explain to kids and teach them lessons about grown-up life. She believes you can explain work to them in a way that makes sense in their own terms. School-aged children know what homework and responsibility are, and *they will learn from how you handle yours how they should handle theirs.*

The periods of imbalance are not going to last forever. But, Angela believes, if you don't figure out a way to allow for this shift in priorities from time to time, you "are killing your soul with guilt and worry" and, sadly, sometimes even questioning why you were blessed with children in the first place. It does not need to be that way. Being a mother and a career woman can work in wonderful and harmonious ebbs and flows of joy, passion, and successes, she believes.

The roadblocks to creating a thriving business are real. Angela's biggest challenge has been burnout. She has been building the business for nine years, and the move to Phoenix was difficult for many reasons. But she approached it in a deeply spiritual way, with prayer and by taking a much-needed breather. She reflected on the term *recreation* and notes it is literally the act of "re-creating," or a chance to rebuild yourself. She admits it is harder for women who are employees to recreate often, but it is critical for entrepreneurs to do so due to the nature of the job. Employees have the fear of missing a meeting or disappointing the boss, but she argues that everyone needs a real break once in a while so that they can take the time to reenergize and get rest.

She loves the book *Don't Sweat the Small Stuff...and It's All Small Stuff* because it puts everything into perspective. "Any perception that you are in control of your life is not real," she says. One of the great benefits of taking a break is the chance to really experience gratitude by slowing down to smell the roses. I was happy that she arrived at this point, because few of the others I have interviewed have done so. I believe gratitude is central to our ability to be happy and successful, and we'll talk about it more in chapter 10, but Angela approached it from another angle— that of faith.

She said you cannot experience real gratitude "if you don't know who brought you to the dance!" She continued, "God has done all of this for you. You are a part of it, of course, but he did it. You must give the glory to God first, however you choose to do so—publicly or privately." She speaks these words of her truth with such conviction. She concluded this point by saying, "Believing that success comes only from themselves is a burden only nonbelievers have." That is a perspective I had not considered before, but I understand what she is saying and admire how her faith can carry her in this manner.

As with many of the women I have talked to for this project, the benefit of 20/20 vision always seems to come with hindsight. Angela talked quite a bit about how she might approach things differently. Goal setting is a big one, and others I have spoken with echoed her views. For the first six years, all of her goals were numbers. Revenue numbers. Number of clients. Number of employees. Numbers, numbers, numbers. What she found was that in focusing just on the numbers, she failed to recognize milestones and missed the chances to celebrate other successes along the way.

At one point, she was pursuing an award for "small business of the year" when someone told her Major Mom was a microbusiness. She was crushed. Until she realized that they were looking only at numbers. The panel of judges neither considered how many households they had transformed nor how many employees were in their dream careers. They did not give proper weight to the vision and mission of Major Mom.

With the move to Phoenix and the burnout running high, Angela got a business coach who has helped her adjust her perspective. She has redefined success so that she can enjoy the journey. She stops to spike the ball at little victories now. She celebrates those little victories with her family to reinforce the notion that it is not all about the numbers. She turned back to her faith and heard God telling her, "It'll be on my timing, baby girl." So she tries to focus on missions accomplished and baby milestones. She says, "I held myself to such high standards that I robbed myself of the joy of celebrations because I was not there yet." She is committed to not doing that anymore. Just recently, she celebrated their biggest payroll in nine years and numerous other milestones. Ahhhh…so much more fun to stop and enjoy victories along the way—big and small.

In Angela's case, her boots are on the ground and her eyes are to the heavens as she lets faith guide her. Not everyone is going to have this approach, but I think it is important to share for all of us to recognize that faith can be central to your life, and you can still operate in the dog-eat-dog world of business happily and on your own terms. Major Mom does.

Sue Kenfield

Sue Kenfield exudes a quiet confidence. As I said when I started this book, I wanted to find everyday women who are in my area from whom to draw inspiration. Sue lives close by, and we met at the chamber of commerce. She is unique among the women I am profiling here because she never married; however, that is not a huge differentiator or that important to this book. It's just that she offers a different perspective from that of all the others featured here.

There are some who are no longer married, but Sue has always been on her own, which is brave too. She does not have the backup of a second income or someone else's insurance, so career decisions she has had to make have had that much more impact. Her conversation with me about work and life was quite a bit more philosophical than that of the others as she emphasized "stepping into authenticity" and "stepping away from that which does not serve you."

Sue's story underscores the importance of knowing yourself and understanding your priorities. She had a dynamic career for many years in training for the medical industry. She also pursued a master's degree in psychology at one point, with the idea that she might want to be a therapist. She found that not to be the right path; however, her education allowed her to further develop her expertise in the area of challenging human dynamics, which she helps her customers improve through her consulting and coaching work. So she has developed a varied background with strengths in several areas.

What she realized as she was going through the training and working and exploring new options was that it was vital to "move beyond the pathology of the past" and that for her to find happiness and success, she was going to need to focus on the now. She really examined the question, "What do you want different in your life?" Knowing that change is an ongoing part of life, she was not afraid of it but wanted to make the right choices for herself. She knew she was good at helping others. What could she change to bring herself more satisfaction?

In the course of exploring options, Sue also became a licensed spiritual counselor. She came to understand how "negative emotions separate us from the Creator." She considered herself someone who loved to be engaged but also looked at that in the context of addictions. Being a workaholic is an addiction of sorts, and that "only takes away the power from within ourselves." Sue was an expert at helping others manage negativity and come back to the center, so she needed to be able to do this for herself. She said that, at the core, we are all perfect and complete, so there must be a way to restore that balance.

She was working too hard. She was living on airplanes and in airports. Because she did not have a family waiting for her at home, she was able to throw herself headlong into her work. However, she knew she was out of balance and needed to change something. She finally approached her employer and asked if she could relocate from the Bay area of California to Denver. There was great access to the whole country from Colorado, and it would cut her travel time down considerably. The company agreed, and Sue sold her home and moved to Colorado to gain new perspective and enhance the balance in her life. Eventually, she took on a position in sales so she could anchor herself more in Colorado and achieve more balance. Things began to align themselves for her again, and life was coming into better focus through these changes.

It worked! Sue found time in Colorado to "fill the well back up" and felt that she was finally able to keep herself whole. She moved to an area outside of the city where there were great trails and places to walk, bike, meditate, and relax. She found that she had grown into balance. Now all she had to do was figure out how to scale this into something she could maintain so that she could sustain her newfound sense of wellness.

She decided to start her own company on the side called See It Thrive and began with smaller projects. When the time was right, she was able to leave the full-time corporate job completely, and now she works on her own. It is not easy, and she still does travel a fair amount, but the quality of life she enjoys and her ability to engage in the community make it worthwhile.

Sue's passion in her work is helping leaders motivate others, and she does that in much the same way she helped herself. She said, "Helping leaders understand themselves is the first step to helping them lead." She loves working with groups over time. As she said, "Watching the breakthrough is amazing, and transformation is gratifying." Ultimately, she said she is "supported by the gifts I was endowed with. Success then is alignment with those gifts."

I believe that is such a profound statement. I once found an anonymous quote on a decorative tile that said, "What you have is your gift from God. What you do with it is your gift back to him." While the intention for this book is not to be overly spiritual or religious, I do believe this is true. It falls in line with the following notion: "To whom much is given, much is expected." (Luke 12:48)

Although Sue and I did not really drill down on this idea, I believe she would agree. One thing she did say that really resonates not only with me but also with all of the stories in this book is this: "Step into doing what you want and what you were made to do, and opportunity shows up." That is a key takeaway from this book, I hope. She also said, "When you jump, the net will appear." I know that is hard to believe and even harder to do, but it has proven true time and time again.

Now, neither she nor I would say to jump impetuously. You cannot have a knee-jerk reaction, make a rash decision without any forethought or planning, and assume it will all go smoothly. However, you can change anything in your life that is within your control, and most things are within your control.

As Sue said, "Faith is a challenging thing to have sometimes when you are balancing pursuing your dreams and paying your bills." But she had it and she did it. I had it and I did it. All of the women in this book struggled with this issue and have landed on their feet. And all of the women in this book are just like you and me. Everyday women with everyday lives who have made changes so that they could pursue the things that mattered most to them—whatever that was.

Sue said that as she was hitting the wall with the corporate job, "My soul felt like I was suffocating." I know that feeling. Most people have felt it at some point, but if you feel like that all of the time, you owe it to yourself to change something. You are the only one who can!

We talked about the difference between her experience and mine, with and without a family to be accountable to. Sue said, "It's a really powerful thing to rely on yourself, and it is a powerful thing to rely on others." That is true. It has been challenging for me, through both transitions I have made with my family, to not be contributing financially to the same degree that I used to. I find it uncomfortable.

At the same time, however, the choice to change my work situation has freed me to help and to carry more of the burden at home, which is a blessing of its own.

Trusting someone to help support you, if you are used to supporting yourself, is a challenge. But you can do it. And you can trust yourself completely, as Sue did, which allowed her to finally slip into her dream. It starts, of course, as I have said before, with the true belief that you can do it.

"Confidence in your own ability to care for yourself is essential," as Sue said. But that does not mean that you have 100 percent unwavering confidence. Few of us really have that. Rather, it is a prevailing belief in yourself with confidence louder than doubt, courage bigger than fear, and the goal better than the reality of your current situation. The right combination of those factors can propel you. You just have to follow your intuition, listen to your gut, and refuse to give up.

Sue said the key for her was knowing what motivated her. I agree. You need to discover what makes you want to get up and go. What is it that gives you the most joy and satisfaction? Now, clearly, work is not all sunshine and rainbows. Please note, I am intentionally not talking about "following your passion." I believe that term has become so overused and that it diminishes what really happens in real career changes that work.

I believe you have to dig deep and be honest with yourself about what you like, what you are good at, and what is realistically possible for you (maybe incrementally over time, if it is a really big goal), and then you have to put one foot in front of the other and walk the walk. Following your heart or your passion sounds too much like something transformative with parted heavens and wings to me. Real change in the real world is more of a march, I think, than a flight.

Sue said that if she could give her twenty-five-year-old self advice, it would be this: "Trust yourself more." Truly, almost every person I spoke with for this book and in conversation about the book answers that question the same way. Trust yourself. Be brave. Go ahead and try. Believe you can.

Sue added, "Trust your inclinations, and trust those feelings that sometimes burst forward. Stop second-guessing yourself." Also, she and the others I spoke with all wish they'd had the courage to believe in themselves much sooner. As Sue said, "I believe everything shows up when you really need it."

When asked whom she admires, Sue said she admires those who actively serve others—people like Dr. Martin Luther King, Lady Diana, Margaret Thatcher, and John Kennedy. People who "ask not" inspire her. Those who work in service of a higher good are the people she looks up to. She believes independence equals freedom and that we must all try our best all the time. "We were never sent here to get it all right," she added. I think she is spot on. Effort matters. Something is better than nothing.

Sue's story inspired me. Her perspectives were deeper than those of some, and she made me think a lot about bigger questions. I was not sure how to retell this and do it justice. I hope I have. Her story is just that of one woman looking life in the eye and making the best of it for herself. It's not a perfect journey, but as she added, "Some of the dark night of the soul experience is necessary to emerge well and stronger." The issue, she said, is always whether we choose to get back on top and ultimately learn and grow from every experience.

Finally, like several others I spoke to, she reminds us that we have to "acknowledge the little successes." In her words, "Take time off to celebrate all that is good and count your blessings...even if you have to be brief and move on."

CHAPTER 10

Real Gratitude

Talent is God-given. Be humble. Fame is man-given. Be grateful.
Conceit is self-given. Be careful.
—JOHN WOODEN

As we come to the last chapter in this journey, I want to end on optimistic and inspirational notes without getting too touchy-feely, keeping it all pragmatic. Last words are funny things; done correctly, they resonate like the sound of a beautiful bell when the note lingers in the air. Done poorly, they can suck the life out of a roomful of people. The goal is to end on a high note and send the readers off on their journey with renewed spirit and focus. The only way I know to do that is to end with a chapter about gratitude.

Every single woman I interviewed in this book expressed gratitude for her life and her work. I am not a fan of the word *lucky* because it is too secular and fickle for my taste. I believe we are blessed with what we have and what we do with it. I have said that here before. In fact, I think we are obligated to optimize the gifts we have been given as a means of magnifying the power of the gifts. Untapped talent, energy, and passion are wasted, and that is the worst kind of waste.

I also believe that coming to understand those gifts within yourself is the first step toward changing whatever you need or want to change to recognize a more authentic life. You owe it to yourself to discover what you can do. Then you can decide what you want to be. The choice is yours alone.

The greatest gift of the process, though, is the feeling you will have during that "aha" moment when you realize—or accept—what you can become. To be clear, it may not be wildly different from who you are now. It may not require cataclysmic change. Maybe you are on the right path, and a bit of introspection and adjustment will just give you greater satisfaction and happiness. Or maybe you do need a big change. But until you take the time to slow down and figure that out, you will not be able to come into the fullness of true gratitude for everything you have been given, including the gift to achieve. God does not give us "stuff"; he gives us talent, and we make choices. I believe that with my whole being.

When we take the time to look around and see all that lies before us, and all that lies within us, how can we not be grateful? It is incredible. It is also relative. Many people with humble lives achieve greatness or do amazing things. At the same time, many people with vast resources at their disposal do nothing notable. Believe me, I understand it is easy to coast in life and live on autopilot. I have done it at times. During periods such as this current one, in times of inspiration and high motivation, I look at those instances of inactivity and cringe at the time I have wasted, at the energy or inspiration I didn't manage to pull forward. Then I have to forgive myself and move on.

Every single day is a chance to start over and try again. Every single day offers us the chance to look around, take stock, put our feet on the ground, and get up and do something meaningful for ourselves or for others. We have renewed opportunity every single day. The question is, what will we do with it? And do we realize how lucky we are to have that day?

Gratitude is the secret sauce that turns everything into a better version of itself as we go. Gratitude turns an exhausted mother into a woman filled with joy as she sees her children drift off to sleep. Gratitude turns the overextended business leader into someone who recognizes the depth of the personal and professional friendships that she enjoys every day. Gratitude helps us appreciate the little house (or the big one) as we write out the mortgage check and grumble. Gratitude motivates us to save for retirement or college with a heart full of joy that we have anything to save. Gratitude turns want into satisfaction. Gratitude says with an abundant spirit, "This is enough for me, and I am happy."

I would like to write a whole book on this topic someday, but for now, this little chapter will have to do. I end with my interview with Christa Reich-Morris. Christa's story is fascinating; I may not have done it justice here, but hopefully I have captured her spirit. Christa is retired now and offers the perspective and wisdom that come with life's experiences. Our conversation was casual and drifted from topic to topic, but it ended with the subjects of gratitude and authenticity and respect. Among all of the things she now values, those rank high for Christa. So I thought I would let her story close us out for now.

Christa Reich-Morris

Back to the idea of getting some multigenerational influence in this book, I have also looked to women I know and admire who are at later stages of their careers than I am, such as Debra Fine and Paula Wiens. When I was making my list of target interviews, Christa Reich-Morris came to mind right away.

Christa is a lovely, elegant woman whom I met through my Rotary Club. She is now retired from her career in advertising and media buying. She was also the first woman president of our Rotary Club, which is celebrating its thirtieth anniversary this year (2015). Christa stood out to me right away partly because of her demeanor and grace and partly because she is such a clear leader. I have known her for about four years, but it was this book that gave me the excuse to invite her over for an interview so that I could learn more about her life. As expected, it was a fascinating conversation.

Every once in a while, I meet women who are striking for their self-determination. Christa reminded me a lot of my mother-in-law, Mary Claire DeCoste, who is now ninety-three and also has a fabulous story to tell. Christa is not that old, mind you, but she is a standout like my mother-in-law for the fact that she knew what she wanted to do and in what direction—literally—she wanted to go from a very young age and at a time when few women did anything unconventional or without the approval of their families.

Christa grew up in Germany as a bright and motivated young woman. She did not know exactly what she wanted to do, but she did know that she wanted to learn English. Her father would not let her study in England until she was twenty-one, so she had to wait, but as soon as she was able, it was off to England she went. She returned to Germany and lived in Dusseldorf (which she also called "drizzle dorf," as it was always raining). She had replied to an advertisement seeking bilingual employees in an advertising agency, which was where her love for advertising began. She was happy to be working and earning a living on her own.

One day, she recalled, looking into the distance over my shoulder as she spoke, when she was in her office, a friend she had met in England showed up unexpectedly and looking radiant. Literally, suntanned and happy, she told Christa that she had moved to California in the United States. "There," she said, "the sun is always shining." The seed was thereby planted!

I am sure there are a few details missing, but Christa was soon on her way to California. She ended up going "via New York" as she said; at least she was getting closer. Over the years, she did finally get to California. She always found work. As she put it, "The Americans simply would not learn German," so there was ample demand for her skills. She did work in some secretarial roles over the years and back in some small and large agencies.

Eventually, she married. Her husband was the food and beverage manager for an airline, so from California they were transferred to Syracuse and then to Phoenix, and finally they landed here in Denver. At some point along the way, their marriage ended. Ever self-reliant, Christa continued to work and support herself without too much difficulty.

Over the years, though, she said in retrospect, she learned some lessons. She, like many, faced discrimination as a woman in the advertising business. (As she told the stories, I kept thinking of *Mad Men*.) There were some cultural adjustments, of course, but ever resilient, she does not linger on negative memories.

Christa does not chalk up her success to luck, exactly, but maybe the right combination of serendipity and determination. She believes that the right circumstances seemed to present themselves when needed and that she was fortunate enough to recognize them and capitalize upon them. (Sounds like Susie Wargin's quote about opportunity and preparation.) I asked if she had aspired to the success she ultimately achieved, owning her own firm, and she said, "No, not really. At least not until it was right there in front of me. Then, of course, I wanted it to be successful. And it was."

It is not that she had a lack of ambition, not at all. Rather, it seems from listening to her talk about her career and life choices that because there were no role models or even the perceptions through most of this of glass ceilings and barrier breaking, she just followed the path she was blazing without realizing it.

I asked her if she was a feminist, and she did not feel that she was. She did not have the time or inclination to burn her bra. She was working. After she left that afternoon, Christa sent me an e-mail that said, in part, "It occurred to me...that I am much less introspective about planning the next steps in my life than many other people are. I guess I am always so busy that I don't stop and give things a lot of thought—I just go—and was fortunate that almost everything fell nicely into place along the way."

I think that is perhaps an oversimplification mixed with the optimism of a selective memory. Many of us have this, I believe. Most of us do not choose to dwell on sad or difficult times. Even if we remember them, our own highlight reels have a rosy filter most of the time, it seems. Such is the case for Christa. She tells the story as if it were all easy.

As it played out, Christa never had children. She was married twice. Her first husband was a good man, and she adored her second husband, who has passed away. She still lives in the house they bought together, and she is still active and vibrant and stalwart and funny and optimistic.

When I asked her about lessons learned, she said she had learned in her life to be very careful and to deal with men, in particular, with caution because they usually hold the chips. She acknowledges the differences between men and women and how we interact with one another but does not overemphasize these issues as a hindrance. There are simply differences.

As I mentioned, she did not believe she had role models, exactly, but she did mention someone she admired—a woman in New York named Mary Wells Lawrence, a talented and successful advertising executive in New York. She was credited with being the first woman CEO of a company on the New York Stock Exchange, and some say she is responsible for the "I 'heart' New York" tagline, among many things. Christa did not remember her for her work but rather for one small action.

As Christa recalled, Mary Wells was shopping in New York and ran across a rare food store that sold a particular kind of pepper (as in spice) that someone she knew would love. Wells stopped and bought it and surprised the recipient, who did not even know Wells was aware of her interest in the item. To many this may not be a particularly compelling story, really, but to Christa it was. She said she thought it was amazing that even as busy and well-known as Wells was at that time, she stopped to do a kind gesture for someone she did not even know that well.

Christa said the story has always stuck with her; one can never be too big or too busy or too successful to be thinking of others, to be grateful, and to show generosity. She said that she could never admire someone she did not respect, and that story of Mary Wells Lawrence made her respect and admire her for her humanity and kindness.

After a lifetime of work in a demanding industry, Christa ultimately seems to have stepped away from the world of work with her heart still full. Her focus on doing good work in the community, supporting friends and fellow Rotarians through difficult times, and keeping people at the forefront of what she does is astonishing. She does so much more than she needs to do at this stage of the game. She is an inspiration to me and could be to all she meets. She is just another "woman next door," but she embodies all the best principles of accomplishing and living in gratitude. These are principles to which I also try hard to adhere; I think they help us keep our feet on the ground *and* keep appropriate perspective when things hit the fan.

When I got married in 1999, Sarah Ban Breathnach's book called *Simple Abundance* was popular. It had a huge influence on me and my thinking at the time. In general, the perspective it put forth is that if we come from a perspective of gratitude, over time, we can change our approach to just about everything. It came with a companion journal in which the owner was to write five things every day for which she was grateful. I kept this journal going without interruption for two years. (This is an excellent exercise, by the way. If you did buy a journal to take notes as you read this book, keep going. Try writing down three to five things for which you are thankful every day. It will change your perspective too.)

Looking back on it now, those were challenging times for me professionally. I had begun a period of instability in my career, jumping from firm to firm for various reasons, mostly trying to chase clients. I was newly married, so that was good, but the pressure of work was enormous, and I was commuting long hours to and from our little place by the beach and into Los Angeles and Century City for most of that time. Sometimes all I could think of to be thankful for was a pretty sunset and the Chardonnay that Paul had waiting for me at home. Once I wrote that I was thankful for mashed potatoes. So, you see, it was not a gargantuan work of literary superiority, but it was authentic. I was grateful for those things and more. And after tracking that for two years, I really could see how blessed I was. It changed my way of thinking.

Each of us must find a way to do this. Gratitude is an attitude, and if you are constantly looking for the good, you will see it—just as much as the opposite is true. Being truly thankful for the people, things, circumstances, and adventures that life throws at us is enormously helpful.

Gratitude inspires optimism and kindness. Gratitude neutralizes fear and self-doubt. Gratitude is also infectious and can change the people around you as much as it changes you. Even gratitude for difficult and challenging times makes a difference. What is it they say? "That which does not kill you makes you stronger."

Obviously, one never feels that way in the throes of hard times, but in hindsight, gratitude heals many wounds and makes the scars tougher.

In the end, we are what we make ourselves. We look at the real world with strength, confidence, and optimism. Hopefully, we have a new resolve now through the stories and inspirations here to move forward—one step or one leap at a time—and march toward our happiest, best selves. Our real selves.

Afterword

This may be one of the most climactic moments I have ever experienced. The book is finished. I have been working on this idea since early 2014. It is May 15, 2015, and here it is. Complete. I am so excited!

For this book, I put together a wish list of thirty women I wanted to feature. There are only fifteen in this volume. Between scheduling and timelines, I could not cover everyone. It is my hope that this book opens doors to more. I have twenty-eight different ideas already outlined, depending on how things go from here.

Please reach out with your feedback to my website (www.GetRealCareerBook.com) or via social media (Facebook.com/GetRealTheBooks or Twitter @kdecoste). Your thoughts and opinions matter to me. Please post reviews for me on Amazon (especially if you like the book) to help drive sales. This has been a labor of love, and every bit of support is welcome.

It is my hope to do additional writing on various industry verticals as well as for different target audiences. I also hope that *Get Real, Ladies* will take on a life of its own and that I will be able to expand my reach, scaling myself from working one-on-one with individual clients to working with larger groups and in various settings. If you have an idea for how I can be of help to you or your organization, please reach out.

For now, thank you for indulging me by reading this book. I hope there will be many more! In the meantime, practice keeping it real, and when in doubt, just try!

Additional Information
about Featured Women

Dr. Chris Linares	**Lone Tree Family Practice**
	www.LoneTreeFP.com
Paula Wiens	**Paula Wiens, PR**
Nealene Orinick	**Neale Orinick**
	www.NealeOrinick.com
Melissa Risteff	**Couragion**
	www.Couragion.com
Vickie Thomas	**Thomas Group Solutions**
	www.ThomasGroupSolutions.com
Susie Wargin	**Susie Wargin**
	www.SusieWargin.com
Kimberly Alexander	**Kimberly Alexander, Inc.**
	www.KimberlyAlexanderInc.com
Angel Tuccy	**Experience Pros**
	www.ExperiencePros.com
Avie Rosacci	**Tony's Market**
	www.TonysMarket.com
Debra Fine	**Debra Fine**
	www.DebraFine.com
Michele Gross	**CAS-ual Friday Stamps**
	http://www.cas-ualfridaysstamps.blogspot.com

Jillian Gibbs	**APR**
	www.APRco.com
Angela Cody-Rouget	**Major Mom**
	www.MajorMom.biz
Sue Kenfield	**See It Thrive**
	www.SeeItThrive.com
Christa Reich-Morris	**Retired**

About the Author

Kim DeCoste is a career management and communication consultant in the Denver area. Her particular area of expertise is professional development, planning for work transitions, and recruiting.

Her firm, DeCoste & Associates (www.DeCosteAssociates.com), was launched in 2007. She has recently completed a term as vice president and editor-at-large for a magazine and media start-up company called ICOSA. Prior to that, she was the Director of Career Services at Colorado Technical University's Denver campuses. She also worked in online education and as a technical recruiter for a number of years in Los Angeles prior to relocating to Denver in 2000.

Kim is active in the South Denver Metro Chamber of Commerce, chairing several committees, including one for the expansion of the Cleantech Open (CTO), Rocky Mountain (www.CleanTechOpen.org), for three years, helping to find, fund, and foster clean tech start-ups. CTO alumni have raised in excess of $800 million to date. She is active in STEM education, Women in Business, and Business Leaders for Responsible Government.

Kim is the recipient of the Chamber's 2011 Extraordinary Leader of the Year Award and is a two-time Brian Vogt Leadership nominee. She has also been active in various volunteer leadership roles at her son's school and in the Douglas County School District. Finally, she is currently serving on the Denver Southeast Rotary board of directors as the chair of public relations.

Kim holds a bachelor's degree from the University of California, Santa Cruz, in language studies (German and Spanish) and an MBA in e-commerce from Jones International University.

Kim and her husband, Paul, have lived in Highlands Ranch, Colorado since 2001. Their son, Stephen, is an excellent student who enjoys baseball, wrestling, martial arts, and traveling with his mom and dad, especially if there is good food involved.

Made in the USA
Lexington, KY
21 September 2015